LIVE Y C.H.O.S.E.N LIFE

"How to Stop Existing and Start Living"

SAJ ZAFAR

DISCLAIMER

Author: Saj Zafar
Title: Live Your C.H.O.S.E.N Life

ISBN: 978-1999620110
Category: SELF-HELP/Personal Development/General Publisher: Breakfree Forever Publishing.

Loving Ourselves through the process of owning our story is the bravest thing we will ever do

-Brene Brown

For my parents
&
Seemab, Ryaan & Ayaan

CONTENTS

INTRODUCTION

I spent my early life desperately trying to escape the life I had. Deep down, I knew there was more than the little that was expected of me because I was born a female. I also knew as I gained knowledge through education and television, trying to make sense of the world, there was a different life that I wanted to be a part of, albeit that I had no clue at that time what that looked like. All I knew was that it was a life that's very different from the one I was living.

My earliest fantasies were about 'leaving home,' living an independent life. Even at the tender age of seven, I had worked out that the life I was destined to live was a far cry from the one I was born into. I hung on to the belief that it didn't matter who I was a Pakistani Muslim female being raised in a western country. I like everyone on this earth, had the right to live a life of my own choosing. It is this belief that kept me going and never giving up in my moments of darkness, hopelessness, and rawness.

Sadly, long after I broke free, I found that I was still bound to my past. The very experiences that caused me pain and suffering continues to haunt, influence, and shackle me.

It took me years before I understood that despite my freedom, I hadn't found happiness nor contentment. I didn't appreciate that my earlier experiences had caused damage, left inadequacies which fueled poor choices, leaving me on many occasions, misunderstood, alienated, and vulnerable. The turning point for me was the realisation that I *had broken free, but not been set free.*

It was only through the process of healing and self-discovery that I learnt that my past was still part of me as much as my present. Whilst this is okay for some, for many like me, it is the very thing that stops us from moving forward and *living our chosen life.*

Elizabeth Gilbert seems to agree. In *Big Magic*, she encourages us to develop a "fierce sense of personal entitlement" — not the idea that the world owes us anything, but that we have a right to be here, on this planet, and to pursue our dreams. I so agreed with what she said in one chapter: you will never be able to create anything interesting out of your life if you don't believe that you're entitled to at least try. Creative entitlement doesn't mean behaving like a princess, or acting as though the world owes you anything whatsoever. No, creative entitlement simply means believing that you are allowed to be here, and that — merely by being here — you are allowed to have a voice and a vision of your own."

Many of us, remain stuck in the past because of our need for certainty. Certainty is one of the six basic human needs and is fundamentally about survival. It's frightening to step into the unknown. It's difficult to be vulnerable. And it can be overwhelmingly uncomfortable to have that sense of uncertainty about what lies ahead. So we hang on to the past - because even if it's steeped in pain, it's what we are familiar with and what we feel certain about. However, continuous pain means continuous damage.

I learnt that if I continued as I was, then there would be a huge cost not only to the way I chose to live my life, but also for my relationships and ultimately the choices I made. It is far easier when you've been doing it for so long, that you continue as you are because you can't imagine it any other way.

However, I have also learnt that your life journey is like any other; if you don't have a destination, you don't have direction, and having no direction will only lead you to drift along hoping, praying, and dreaming that one day you may just wake up and find yourself where you want and hope to be. The downside of that approach is *we only have one life.*

Over the past decade, I have worked and coached hundreds of women from all walks of life. I have found that it doesn't matter who we are or where we are from. We have an innate desire to find our purpose, to serve and seek to live the best version of ourselves. However, for many of us, life happens and gets in the way, and soon we find that our state of busyness, convenience, and comfort serves us to maintain the status quo. We dare not dream, we dare not desire, we dare not think I could, I should, I would, just in case we find ourselves embroiled in regret, shame, fear, all the feelings that we have learnt to mask and or keep buried deep within.

For many, that is fine, and so it should be as long as it is a personal choice. However, for others, the reminder of our unfulfilled dreams, desires, ambitions, aspirations, have a habit of resurfacing, most likely in times of vulnerability and difficulty, reminding us that there is more to life than this. Overridden with guilt and ingratitude, we shake off these thoughts and return to our here and now... till next time. There is always a next time.

Maybe the starting point of any change has to be acceptance. Acceptance that until now we have allowed ourselves to exist, to fall prey to the expectations of others, and allowed ourselves to take on beliefs, values, and attitudes that compel us to conform. *And here we are now not as the person we ever set out to be... but the person who we have become.*

Change is often scary and uncomfortable. Change means letting go of the old and replacing with the new. That requires time, effort, energy, and the know-how. It is no surprise that, as women, we continue to remain as we are. Whilst it may not be the right choice, it definitely remains an easy one.

I read somewhere that 'the woman who moves forward towards change with most ease and grace is the woman who is willing to tell herself the fundamental truth. She's the woman ready to admit: I am no longer willing to settle, I am not willing to do this anymore...

Have you ever wondered why life seems easy for some people? They're confident and in control, and seem to go through life with relative ease.

The truth is, there is no secret, nor is it rocket science. They are focused on what they need to do and who they need to become to create their desired life. They are following some simple steps and are committed to being the best they can be.

So if it is that simple, why is it that over 95% of people do not live their desired dream; instead, they continue to exist and live a life of compromise.

What I discovered through my own self-discovery journey and coaching many women is that it isn't just about setting and achieving goals. Getting what you want is the easy part, knowing what you want is the most difficult part.

Even though once you are lucky enough to figure that out, yet why is it that so many of us still do not manage to live our dreams and achieve our aspirations.

It is only when I sat down and decided to search for the answer to these questions that I realised that I had been approaching it the wrong way. Whilst my goals were always clear, what I needed to focus on what got in the way. It is only when I stopped to focus on this that things started to make sense.

I also realised that everything I had used to coach the women was absent from my own life. Here, I was 'fixing' others when all the time I was neglecting to help myself.

I have to confess; my aha moment was a sheepish acceptance that I so wished that I had taken the time to make this discovery before now.

Life is made up of moments. Moments are opportunities. How you approach the moment and what you choose to do with it is what will create a momentum. It is this momentum of gathered moments that are your so-called life.

I spent a lifetime waiting to be rescued until I realised that I had to be my own rescue. Once I had this realisation, I began to learn and experience the what and how.

I have written this book to inspire, encourage, and motivate you to continually be the best you can be. By maintaining this focus, you too will begin to create the kind of life you have been dreaming of - one that is filled with your own definitive success and happiness. My purpose is to support you as you strive to be the best that you can be - in both your personal and professional life. As you read this book, I hope you will start your own personal journey of self- discovery. The journey ahead will not be easy, and there will be times this book will take a shelf life. However, I hope that when you feel the need, you can pick it up, like an old trusted friend, and refer to it, at different times, over the course of your life. I believe that at some point, the time will be right and you will take the steps and decisions to *live your chosen life.*

The book is divided into different sections, each chapter devoted to a layer of understanding. Today, I am pleased that I am able to share the lessons learnt with you, hopefully through this book. I hope as you work through the book, you will find a simple, tangible process that you can pick up and apply. Not only will you understand how to set your goals, but you will also learn the things that get in the way of you accomplishing them.

You will also learn how to overcome these obstacles. This combined with learning about the 'true' you, warts and all, rather than the perception you hold of yourself, will you then be able to grow and become a better you.

I have found that it is not until you are prepared to make peace with your past and come to terms with where you have been, who you have become, can you then truly feel empowered to make choices, decisions, to help you to live your chosen life of fulfilment and joy.

I'd love to tell you that the road to your dreams is going to be easy, but we all know that there are times in life when we feel like giving up. Sometimes, those obstacles might be imagined, but at other times they will be very real. Working through the tough times focuses on meeting your challenges head-on and staying on track. Celebrating your success: saving the best for last, the final chapter is about celebrating success and, equally as important, acknowledging all your successes along the way.

After all, living your chosen life is not just a destination, *IT'S A JOURNEY.*

Before you embark on your journey, it may be helpful to know who I am.

MY JOURNEY

I AM NOT WHAT HAPPENED TO ME... I AM WHAT I CHOOSE TO BECOME

September 2001

I look down at my feet, too scared that if I looked up, they would see my nervousness. I could feel all eyes on me, questioning, half guessing how I came to be and why I was here.

The freshly waxed floor shone, but still remained dirty from years of ingrained grime. The stench was just about bearable a mixture of disinfectant and pungent staleness. The September sun seeped boldly through the metal bars of the window, throwing light on the dust particles, which appeared to dance in mid-air. I was losing focus on what was being said. The man speaking, tall but slightly hunched, peering over his glasses at his notes. I looked straight ahead, the sea of crisp white shirts with epilates and stony faces of the men stared back. Motionless, grim, and focused.

Someone once told me that life is made up of moments; good, bad, and indifferent. It didn't matter what the moment was; it was how you approached it that defined you. Either you would rise strong or you could fall and crumble.

This is one of those moments. How I approach this will set the momentum going forward. My heart is beating, and I'm trying to control my breathing. I find myself holding my breath. A habit that I find difficult to shed since childhood. Only letting go when I regain control. I half smile, it is ironically bittersweet and poetic justice that I should find myself here sat in prison after having spent a lifetime, trying to escape and be free.

My life in the main has been full of disappointment and despair.

Intertwined with disempowering cultural beliefs, a misrepresented religion, and having to adhere to a code of conduct that prescribes shame, fear, and guilt, it is no wonder in moments like this that I find myself plummeting into depths of hopelessness. I have to remind myself that, albeit few, there have been moments when I have risen strongly, and it is in those moments that I have felt liberated and elevated.

I hope and pray that, today, I don't fall and crumble as I was too aware of what lay ahead...

My mother tells me that it took her three days to push me out into this world. She remembers that the labour went on forever and in the absence of drugs, epidural, she is still able to recount every contraction. I finally arrived in the early hours of a Tuesday, one late summer. She doesn't know the date or the month or the year. This is not unusual as no one knew how to read and write in the village. It wasn't normal practice to note things down like the time and birth date of your child. The name she gave me is different to the one the world knows me by today. She smiles at the next bit of her story and takes great joy in detailing how huge I was, likened to a little sumo wrestler, dark in colour, she emphasises this point as those with dark skin are perceived inferior and seen negatively to those that are light skinned, thick hair that curled at the end, eyes shut, fists clenched and lungs that carried my cries to the next village. She goes on to say that there was little cause for celebration around my birth as the family had prayed hard that I be born a boy the second child to my elder sister.

February 1972

It was a cold February when my mother and I travelled from Pakistan to join my father in London, leaving my older sister behind to be cared for by my grandmother. We travelled to a small mining town in South Yorkshire, one of the first Asian families to settle.

My early memories are compounded by my mother's loneliness, her humming at the sink, tears trickling down her face, and often hiding her face into a black and white photograph of a pretty young light-skinned girl who she called her daughter...

Over the next four years, I was joined by my two brothers, which was a relief as it was a good distraction for my mother and provided her with the respite from the pressure that she had endured from not giving birth to sons.

Life was pretty uneventful until I started school. The first day at school is usually an important and exciting milestone for most children. Sadly, mine was a far cry from that.

I stood at the school gates looking at the sea of children and parents, desperate to hold my mother's hand, but my mother was neither affectionate nor tactile. Instead, I stood next to her, gripping the pram handle for dear life, watching on, knowing this was the place where she would leave me. I saw the other mothers lean down and kiss their little ones. I looked across to mine, where she was busy adjusting my brother. Sensing that I was staring at her, she looked over at me and told me that she would come back later and pick me up. With that, she untightened my fingers and slightly pushed me away in the direction of the school. I watched her push the pram and walk away into the distance, not once looking back. I turned and reluctantly walked into the playground. Nothing had prepared me with what I saw. My mother had failed to tell me that all the other children would be different to me in colour, pale with light hair and light eyes. They spoke a different language, one that sounded similar to the people on TV. The adults were a larger version of the children, all pale in their funny-looking colourless clothes and grim faces.

It was no surprise, feeling like an alien and being treated as such by both children and the teachers alike that I soon found myself crying at a moment's notice, so much that soon, I became the brunt of everyone's frustration. Sadly, I didn't make friends; instead, I became a point of fascination as the other children tried to make sense of who I was. I learnt to fight before I learnt to write as the other children poked fun at me, pulled my long oily braid and tried to smear the black kohl from my eyes. They would twitch their noses when I passed them to remind me that the strong fragrances of my mother's cooking were heavily embedded into my clothes, causing distaste and further alienation.

Inwardly, I died a thousand deaths wishing and praying that someone would come and rescue me. Sadly, no one came...

July 1978

It was a late summer evening, my brother and I were hard at play with the local gang of boys. My father had been absent for a whole day and night. Mother was unusually quiet and preoccupied, which was good as it made it much easier for me to escape my housework duties and enjoy playing cricket with the local boys who were much older but tolerant of me being a girl and young. Being the only female and the youngest had its disadvantages, as I was always volunteered to carry the heavy wickets and bat, never allowed to bowl and allocated to field from the furthest point where the ball hardly came. However, I didn't mind as I felt almost as though I belonged to the group, albeit on the periphery and I could be me, witty, charming, and hold a ballsy attitude, which most boys respected and envied.

It was late evening and mother, as usual, shouted out through the open back door. My brother and I entered the house with the sole aim to down our food quickly and then return to finish the match. Unfortunately, mother had other plans; she looked exceptionally happy as she told us to wash our hands and gestured us to go inside where we found a pretty young girl sat on the sofa. She looked familiar, but I knew we hadn't met. She looked up and smiled. I stared at her, feeling awkward and clumsy.

Mother asked for us to sit and eat our dinner, which my brother and I did, unusually without any fighting and bickering, all the time sneaking looks at the girl visitor who constantly smiled shyly.

As we approached the end of the meal, I signalled to my brother that we should make a move. My mother was too quick. 'You are not going outside, it's late, and you need to stay here.' Frustratingly and annoyingly, I slowly picked up the dishes from the table, feeling angry that the female visitor had interfered with my evening of play. In the kitchen, I swung around as I realised mother was in pursuit and whispered, signalling towards the stranger. When is she going home?

I'm not sure how I didn't drop the dishes in my hand when my mother responded 'she's not going home, this is her home. She will be staying here; she's your sister.'

Six months later, I sat next to my new found sister and watched her marry our cousin at the age of fifteen. She looked pretty in her blood red outfit and heavy ornate jewellery. I remember looking at her, feeling sorry for her. No sooner had she found her family, she was being palmed off to strangers to set up a new life as a wife, daughter-in-law, sister-in-law, living with an extended family of many… I wondered how she would cope.

September 1981

High school was much bigger and required more time and energy for me to wane off the bullies. Sadly, I became the target of a group of girls, beautiful blonde girls, with short miniskirts, perfect hair, perfect smiles, perfect everything. Although by now, I had a good command of English, albeit colourful, I had built a reputation for retaliation and taking no crap. This didn't stop them from coming; every day, someone somewhere pushed me, pulled me, provoked me just to see how I would react. I didn't need encouragement as I chose to fight. With time, the fights became bloodier; the bruises became darker and more frequent. However, nothing ever prepared me for the hurt I felt when my mother would comb my hair before I set off to school each day and as the clumps of hair fell, so did the venomous curse from my mother's lips. I would stand still, fighting back the tears and holding my breath until the ordeal was over.

This soon became my daily routine. However, it was not all doom and gloom as more Pakistani families arrived in the town and I soon befriended two Asian girls that I could call friends. They were both pretty, quite dim and conformed to all that was expected of them. They lived by the code of honour, shame, and fear.

You will bring no shame; you will live with humility and honour. This statement was etched and embedded into every brain cell of a girl child. No one dared to question the consequences if one should fail to live and abide by these rules. The constant whispering of stories of those girls who did bring shame and dishonour, and their terrible endings were a deterrent for the rest of us. Most of the girls were sent back to the home country, never to return, others disappeared quietly... then there were those that were made examples of... It is these stories that acted as a reminder and kept us in tow.

If anyone of us did have dreams or thoughts, we knew not to speak them. Stifled by cultural expectations, fear of the consequences, combined with the fear of Allah, kept us in our place.

It was a dark November night, the air was cold, and it was pitch black. I huddled into my coat and picked up pace. Another detention, another late return home. I was running out of excuses, and the anticipated scathing scolding from my mother made me shudder. I decided to take the shortcut via the snicket path, hidden by overgrown bushes and absent of any street light. The snicket path was renowned for attracting sleazy old men in long coats, who were known to pounce out of the bushes and flash their naked bits at women and children. I shook my head at these intrusive thoughts, and half giggled consoling myself that fighting the old man was far easier than feeling the wrath of my mother's curse.

Today had been a difficult day, and I just needed it to be over. I had ended up punching one of the bully's, nearly knocking her out, so much that I scared myself. Girls always fought dirty, pulling hair, biting, scratching. I, on the other hand, had learnt from early on that kicking in the shins followed by throwing a punch to the side of the head, aiming for the ear usually led to the opponent falling over quite quickly, giving me enough time to lay a few more kicks before the playground supervisor turned up to pull me off and reprimand me, on most days with writing a few thousand lines during lunchtime or detention after school. Tonight had been such an evening.

The crisp air hit my face. Suddenly, I hear footsteps, behind me picking up pace and getting closer. I knew it was more than one person. I also knew this was no old man in a raincoat wanting to get his wicked way with me. My heart started to race as I tried to pick up pace, but was not quick enough.

I felt something sharp connect with my shoulder blade. I gasped and swung around. I caught a glimpse of the silver scissors as it was pulled out. I looked on in horror as the girls turned and ran away into the pitch dark evening. I stopped, and for a moment, my head started to swim as I tried hard to control my erratic breathing. I reached over my shoulder with my right hand and felt something warm and sticky. I put it up to my face, the smell of blood hit me and I slowly started to stumble towards home.

I snuck through the front door and ran upstairs to my bedroom. I slowly pulled off my coat, wincing with pain. I saw the lining of my thick duffle coat soaked in red. I peeled off my school jumper and then my blouse. The blood was still gushing. I walked slowly to the bedroom door and listened. There was no one at home. I walked downstairs and dialed my friend's number and whispered for her to come over, urging her to bring first aid supplies. Between us, we managed to stop the bleeding with talcum powder and lots of cotton wool and tape.

A few hours later, I stood in the kitchen, helping my mother prepare the evening meal. I stood on the worktop, slowly rolling the dough into shape, holding my breath as each movement sent a piercing pain through me. I jumped as a drinking glass shattered onto the tiled kitchen floor. I don't have to turn around. I stifle a scream as my mother pulls me to face her. The onslaught of cursing begins. She is screaming and crying at the same time. Reminding me how, once again, I had brought shame to the family... the words tumbled out like venom, and as always, the words hurt more than the punches, kicks, or sharp scissors. I close my eyes and exhale slowly.

I was a few shades darker, taller than the average Pakistani girl, big boned, and not so pretty. However, luckily for me, I was smart, had a brain and was strong in personality. I always stepped up to take responsibility for my family, stepping up and acting as a second mum to my younger siblings, my OCD tendencies made me a great cleaner, and a passion for cooking meant that I nearly possessed all the qualities that a future mother-in-law seeks in her daughter-in-law. This is an important piece of knowledge to hold as marriage becomes a prominent subject when Pakistani Muslim girls reach puberty.

June 1983

Gary, our career teacher who declined to use his second name, an extrovert and outwardly gay rolled his eyes exaggeratedly and let out a deep sigh... 'May I ask why you are here, he looked at me frustratingly with disdain.

I try to explain that, like the other students, I wanted to work over the summer. He arched his eyebrow questioningly, what do you mean? His voice was laden with agitation now... Work experience sir, like everyone else... Another deep sigh. You are not going to go on work experience... It would just be foolish; you would be wasting everyone's time... Exams, work, career;

these things don't happen where you come from... I looked confused...He softened his approach and continued, 'sweetheart, we all know. He looked at me as though he was about to share a secret and slowly in a whisper, slightly leaning forward, he said you know what they are going to do with you... They will marry you off to one of those cousin taxi drivers... You will end up pushing babies out year after year and then living with the clan, cooking and scrubbing. You won't need work experience, lovey, neither will you need exams. I just hope they find someone who can handle you... especially with your reputation, which I must say has settled and surprised us all. With that, he rolled his eyes and turned away dismissively...

It was lunchtime, and the three of us sat on the wall, watching the pretty girls, their arms linked, walking on by, giggling, flirtingly at a group of boys that were watching... they didn't appear to have any care in the world. They looked even prettier and happier today. I spoke slowly, 'I'm thinking of leaving.' There was pin drop silence. After what seemed an eternity, one of them spoke. Leaving, what do you mean leaving? You mean running away. Running away made it sound worse than it was, as though I had no choice. I was talking about an exit plan, a plan that was thought through and executed without getting caught. Defensively, I retorted No. I mean I'm going to leave. Saying it out loud for the first time sounded alien and less convincing. Both giggled nervously. Well, you aren't going to get far, one of them lowered her tone and looked around to make sure no one heard us and whispered, they will catch you, and then they will kill you. You know that, right...

My heart sank as I read the truth in her words. I didn't want to get caught nor killed... She sighed exasperatedly. You know what happens... she lowered her voice so that I barely could hear her... every girl that has attempted to run away is either back home, she gestured with her eyes towards the sky and continued or is... She looked around to make sure no one else can hear the word dead. Please tell me you're not going to do anything stupid. I looked away, already regretting sharing my secret of so long... all these years, I had held onto my dream, living far away near the sea, in a small house full of books. I would drive a car and have a job. I wasn't sure what that was just yet, but it would be proper and important work, that much I knew. I would travel the world and visit America, the land of dreams, the land of beautiful women, good-looking men... just like the TV show Dallas.

I was not going to be like the other girls. Girls who hadn't planned their exit properly. Girls who ran away because they were in love and always made the mistake of getting their lover to help. In most cases, he would get beaten up, she would disappear, and that would be the end of the love story. Arranged marriages had a much 'happier ending.' I told myself I was smart and would plan properly and definitely not share it with anyone. I regretted saying anything to the other two. I tried to seek comfort in the uttered words, wishing them back, but it was too late. Fear captured the back of my throat as I caught my breath...

I know something you don't... I ignored her and wondered why she hadn't gone back to her husband, the novelty of having a 'perfect' sister was wearing thin. She was everything that mother wanted and desired. The comparisons were endless and only fueled jealousy and hate. I prayed that day would soon come when I would long be gone. Then they would see... I wondered if they would miss me... She continued deliberately spicing the conversation, dragging it out and trying her utmost to create suspense. I overheard mum and dad talking earlier today, and they've done it... you're so lucky she rushed on, he's a lovely boy, I like him, he was so good to me... however, it does mean you would have to go back home and live there because he doesn't have a passport. Something snapped as I lunged forward to hit her. She screamed, and mother came running into the room, pulling me off and hitting me at the same time. What is wrong with you? She screamed. I opened my mouth, as hot tears of disbelief fall. Nothing comes out. I withdraw and walk slowly out of the room.

I lay on my bed, sobbing and hurting until I couldn't cry anymore. I slowly pulled out the poster from under my mattress. George Michael looked so beautiful and kind. I stroked his face and closed my eyes, praying someone would come and rescue me...

Three weeks passed, and I slept very little, ate hardly, spoke less, and cried rivers. Nothing changed, I remained engaged to a boy in a far off land, a place that I didn't remember.

It was a late summer evening, and I could hear the children playing outside. I leaned against the half-open window and looked down at them as they played tag running around with not a care in the world. I felt sad. I looked down at the small brown plastic bottle in my hand. I sat on the edge of the bed and unscrewed the cap.

The small round tablets fell onto my hand. I hadn't considered how many I had to take before I would die. I wondered if it was quick. I hoped I would fall asleep and die peacefully. They would find me; they would naturally be upset, but I guessed they would get over it. I shook my head, as this was interfering with what I needed to do. It was no use thinking about them, I needed to think about me, and why it was important that I should die. The plan of escaping seemed unrealistic and impossible.

I felt saddened as, deep down, I wasn't sure if dying was the answer, but it seemed the only way to deal with everything that was happening. Three weeks of refusing food, crying endlessly and constantly hurting hadn't persuaded my parents to call the engagement off. Neither were they too concerned with the idea that I should leave and go to Pakistan to marry a stranger that I had never met.

Poor mother had tried her utmost, fluctuating between being kind to frustratingly becoming angry and threatening to kill me if I didn't do as I was told. Right now, this was the only way. I would make it easier for everyone. I was always in trouble, always causing mother pain, no one liked me, and no one would actually miss me. No, this was the best way and the only way. I sighed as I took the pills and placed a handful in my mouth, immediately spitting them out as the bitter taste caused me to regurgitate. Panicked that I was running out of time and this was not as straightforward as I had planned, I started to swallow two tablets at a time until there were none and the bottle was empty.

I could hear the children still laughing, running in the distant, but nothing was happening. I hid the bottle behind the cupboard and lay on the bed, waiting.

I wasn't sure how long it was before I felt a surge of vomit shoot through me. I leapt and ran into the bathroom. Vile liquid poured out of me, repeatedly. I was perspiring heavily, and there was a shooting pain in my stomach. I leaned against the mirror, which felt cold and provided respite. Then there it was again, the rush of vomit combined with a piercing pain in my stomach. I started to cry... I wanted my mother... I stumbled downstairs, the room was spinning, and then there was nothing. I felt someone tapping my face, and I looked up at my mother, her face full of worry. I can't ever remember being this close to her. I felt guilty and ashamed. I whispered, I'm sorry. Then there was darkness...

I opened my eyes; someone was calling my name, 'listen, lovey, you need to stay awake. Can you do that for me... My eyes felt droopy and heavy, and the voice started to fade. As I fell back into unconsciousness, I knew they were going to save me. Dis- appointingly, I closed my eyes and slowly exhaled.

I tried to force my eyes open, but the light hurt. I could feel someone close by. She looked friendly, her eyes crinkled at the edges, and she smiled. Com' on, poppet, you need to wake up, as she propped up my pillows. The ceiling and the walls were white. I looked down and saw my mother sitting at the end of the bed. She looked tired and worried.

I sensed her standing next to me. Her voice sounded faint as I tried to shut it out. She reminded me of how I had failed her, how I had caused her embarrassment, and everyone was blaming her saying she had no control of me... How I had brought shame, and now everyone knew there was something wrong. Why did I always make it hard for her, why couldn't I just be like my sister? What was wrong with me.... I turned away and let the tears fall.

I stared at the woman sat across in the leather armchair. Her hair was blonde, and her eyes were unsmiling and serious. She occasionally looked up from writing her notes. She finally spoke, mispronouncing my name. I didn't dare correct her. She introduced herself as the Psychiatrist in a matter of a fact voice and continued to ask why I had taken the tablets. I looked at her and wondered if God had sent her to rescue me. I wondered if I told her everything would she help me, take me away, move me into the house, help me get a job so that I could live my life just the way I wanted, eating pizza and being happy. I opened my mouth, wanting to tell her everything, all of my fears, all of my pain, but instead, nothing came out. I zoned out, letting her voice trail in the distance, talking about how social services could help me, but I need to tell her; otherwise, there was very little she could do to help. I looked away and thought about what lay ahead when I returned home back to the life I knew. My legs felt weak, and my hands had turned a shade of pale yellow. This was not how this was supposed to end. When she finished speaking, I slowly turned and wheeled myself out of the room.

June 1985

School had finished, and the summer was bright. I looked at him shyly, feeling awkward. He smiled his gorgeous smile and his brown eyes danced with mischievousness. He reached out and took my hand, which felt hot and clammy. He looked down, leaned over, and whispered reassurances of how it was going to be ok as long as we were together. I believed him. I loved him so much that I felt overwhelmed, my heart pounding as though it was ready to burst out of my chest. We walked hand in hand through the woodland park, and for the next few hours, there were only blue skies, birds chirping and endless naïve conversations full of hope, promise and plans of being together. I looked over at him feeling sad that it was time for me to go. I needed to get back on the bus home, making sure that I reached on time before any suspicion was aroused. I had been lying to my parents about having study days at the college when in actual fact I was seeing him, my first ever love.

We walked slowly to the corner point where I knew he had to leave me. I clung on tightly to his hand before finally letting go. I longingly watched him walk away. I turned to walk towards the bus stop. In my moment of euphoria, I hadn't spotted my father's car parked nearby.

I landed with a bump. Confused and panic-stricken, questions raced through my head. Had my father seen him walk away? How long had he been there watching, waiting? With shaky hands, I opened the back passenger door and slid into the car. He turned, his eyes bulging, his face dark like thunder, his words tumbling out as he roared at me, at the same time pulling his shirt, ripping the buttons. I sunk deeper into the seat, now frightened as I had never seen him like this. The drive home was short but seemed to take forever. My breathing became jagged as we got closer to home not knowing want would happen next.

I walked quickly through the back door with my father at my heels still shouting and screaming. This time at my mother, telling her how he had found me with a boy. I ran upstairs toward my bedroom, but didn't reach in time. I felt something blunt against the back of my head. I swung around to see my father raging with a broomstick in his hand. I saw the stick come down on me as I fell to the floor. He repeatedly hit me and continued to do so. I'm not aware of which happened first; him tiring or my staying still motionless. I heard him retreat. I slowly exhaled.

Several weeks had passed, and no one spoke to me. My meals were brought and left at my bedside. Each day rolled into another, and each day, I wondered if word had got out about my dishonouring act, and if someone was going to come and rescue me. No one came.

I sat up in bed and watched him frame the bedroom window, his back towards me. He couldn't bring himself to look at me. Inwardly, I felt ashamed, and I wished and prayed this was not happening. He spoke slowly and deliberately. He spoke of us leaving for Pakistan to visit his family. Before I could attempt to say anything, he turned and left.

The van door opened as I stepped out. Realising that my four- inch stilettos probably had not been a wise choice of footwear, I followed my father across the large veranda through the double door into the house. The hall was dark and cool. My grandmother looked me up and down disapprovingly through her thick glasses. She sighed frustratingly at my father. He tried to provide her with assurances, that although I didn't speak the language, I did cook, clean, and knew how to pray. Dissatisfied and disappointed, my grandmother accepted the challenge of taking me on.

Six weeks had lapsed, and through rivers of tears and tantrums and refusing to leave my father's side, I ended up alienating myself, drawing wrong attention and becoming the brunt of cruel jokes from the female members of the family. They all approached me with detestation. Word had reached that I had broken the sacred rule and had been caught with a boy... I was now 'marked' forever. Dirty and cheap. I had succeeded in dragging the family name through the mud never to be clean again. I was constantly reminded of how lucky I was that I was not dead. I didn't feel lucky; instead, I felt very unlucky to be alive.

Dawn was breaking, and the early light tried to creep through the netted windows. I felt a presence. I opened my eyes and saw my father sitting on the edge of my bed looking down deep in thought. I stirred so that he would know I had woken. He shot me a glance, and then looked away. Finally, he got up and made his way out of the room and walked up to the garden wall, standing, staring out into space. Barefoot, I followed him slightly confused, but nevertheless pleased. Convincing myself that my punishment was over and we were returning home, I looked forward to seeing my siblings. I would also be seeing mother again, my beautiful, beautiful mum, who I had missed incredibly.

A part of me wanted to jump up squeal and even shout at the top of my lungs, yes, yes, I was going home... He still hadn't turned around, still staring ahead motionless... I then paid attention to what he was saying. The words were slow and deliberate. I'm leaving you here. You will stay here; it will be good for you will learn to become a proper Pakistani Muslim girl. What you did was unforgettable. You're lucky that your uncle is a kind man; he has paid no heed to the stories and is still happy for you to marry his son, not now as you have your studies, but in a few years' time. By then, you will be ready. Your mother and I will then come for your wedding. Till then, I beg you... I never heard the end of his sentence. Slowly, I walked backwards, stifling the lump in my throat, fighting the tears that were burning my eyes and the deafening gush in my head was sending signals to my stomach as I felt a surge of sickness built up. Clasping my mouth, I turned and ran back into my room.

Two years had passed. One evening, I caught my grandmother whispering. The fact she looked over at me every now and then plucked my interest and forced me to pay attention. Something about my naani was ill, and my mother had arrived to see her. Perched on a low stool doing the evening washing of endless pots and pans, a thousand questions raced through my head; why had I not been told? My weekly phone calls, although monitored and brief, had been an opportunity for my mother to share this important news with me. Clearly, if she were visiting Pakistan, she would come and see me and take me home. Instead, the stark truth was she had flown and was with her own mother with no thought to tell me. I hadn't seen her for over two years... I came back quickly to my senses when I realised that I had been holding a glass in my hand and had rubbed it so hard that it cracked. The sharp edge cut across my thumb... I winced as the blood gushed out. I held it under the water tap, watching the blood gush until my hand was turning numb and there was no more pain...

I quickly dressed for school and draped a huge shawl covering my head and half of my face, revealing only the eyes. I gripped the few hundred rupees that I had kept hidden in my school shoes, hoping it would be enough. Picking up my school bag, I exited as usual. Instead of turning right, I took a sharp left and left again and hurriedly half-walked and half-ran to the bottom of the hill where the buses were lined up. The drivers and conductors, simultaneously shouting, calling out their destinations. I held the shawl tight, fear of being recognised and drawing unwanted attention. It was not customary for a young girl to travel alone, unescorted. I had made this trip a few times with naani when she had come and taken me during the school holidays. I approached the dirty peasant looking conductor; he hardly seemed much older than me. I handed him the money and waited for my change. I climbed onto the bus and navigated my way toward a seat where an elderly woman with a huge shopping bag sat, and took my place next to her, hoping that everyone would assume we were together.

The bus travelled for several hours, and soon we reached the outskirts of where I needed to be. I stepped out of the bus, hungry and tired, with other fellow passengers - women, children, and the elderly. The August sun hit me hard, and my lips felt dry and parched. I slowly started to walk across the cobbled wasteland path leading me towards the distant mud houses. I felt a surge of excitement and imagined mother being shocked, but overwhelmingly pleased to see me. She would run towards me and take me in her arms. She had never done that before, but today was different. She hadn't seen me for over two years and by now, most likely had forgiven me for all my wrongdoings... I imagined pushing my head deep into her bosom and inhaling her smell warm and sweet.

I approached the open yard. It was noon, and the sun was at its highest point. Single beds were strategically placed to capture the shade of the trees. I caught sight of a familiar shape, that of my mother lying, fanning herself. I recognised those feet anywhere... my sweet mum... I rushed up to her. Alarmed, she jumped into a sitting position, squinting to focus on the sun. I pulled off my shawl, revealing my face and uniform. Her face changed to concern and panic when she realised it was I who was standing. She continued to fan herself and slowly pulled herself up, standing in front of me. She then came forward; I froze, watching her intently. She took my face in both her hands and kissed both of my cheeks in turn. She then sat down and gestured to the spot next to her.

There were no loving welcome or intimate words of how happy she was to see me. Instead, her voice was lined with concern and slight agitation. Questions stumbled and the imaginary reunion dissipated. I could hear her telling me that I shouldn't have come to see her and by taking matters into my own hand had made matters worse. I stared out to the field, the golden crops all shone like a blanket. There was a slight breeze and time stood still...

Several hours later, my mother bid me goodbye; this time, with my uncle, her half-brother as my escort... ...I don't remember the journey back ...

Weeks had passed, and my mother yet again had become a distant memory. It was mid-morning, and I was deeply engrossed in my house chores. Kneeling down on all fours, I wring the dirty wet cloth and begin to wipe the floor. I didn't mind the cleaning, it kept me occupied and out of trouble. It also allowed me to escape into faraway places, places where the people were kind. They smiled, a place where I belonged, often I would hear his voice, it's going to be ok... a promise that he had not been able to keep. I fought back the tears as I struggled to reconcile the truth of my own tragic love story. I heard he had run away with my best friend, they both had sought help from the local social services and had left town... Unbeknown to me, my mother had walked through the side gate unnoticed, and when she caught sight of me on all fours scrubbing the floor, she paused and decided to watch from behind the pillar.

I finished the veranda and stood up, feeling proud of my workmanship. My next chore was to clean the gutter that ran along- side the house which was full of mud, debris, and leaves. I went and found some carrier bags, and placed them over my hands in order to protect myself from being stung by unknown insects. My stomach turned as I picked up the wet mud, leaves, and sluggish rubbish and placed it in the wheelbarrow. Elbow deep in mud, face smeared sweaty dirty brow and stinking of the gutter is how my mother found me. I couldn't contain my surprise and pleasure. My mother, on the other hand, looked angry; eyes huge and tight-lipped.

It was early dawn as the late night shadows slowly attempted to disappear. I felt someone pull gently on my arm… Mother was sat on my bed, her face close to mine. She whispered that we were leaving and whilst I had been sleeping, she had packed my small suitcase. She told me to wash quickly and quietly as not to disturb the rest of the household. She would go and find a rickshaw to take us to the bus station. I leapt out of bed as though it was filled with hot charcoals. I stopped suddenly in my tracks. It dawned on me that, like a fool, once again, I had got caught up in the moment, racing on. She wasn't going to get a rickshaw; instead, this was her ploy to distract me and leave. She was sending me to the bathroom so she could exit. I would return to find her gone. No, she wasn't going to do that this time. Enough was enough. I turned and ran back to her, taking her hands into mine. I looked at her pleadingly; please, mom, don't leave me, I need to go with you. If you leave me, I will really die… For the first time in my life, my mother took me in her arms and pushed my face into her bosom and whispered, I'm not going to leave you, we will leave together, but we have to be quiet, no one can hear us, so quickly get ready.

We both crept out of the hall and onto the veranda as we made our way to the outer gate. We heard my uncle's voice shout from behind us. We stopped and turned. My heart began to race. I looked over to my uncle who was standing there, tall and angry. His voice boomed. His warning for us not to leave hangs in the air. There was silence, then my mother spoke. I felt her grab my upper arm and squeeze it so hard I'm not sure how I didn't yelp out in pain. She is my daughter, and I am leaving with her. With that, she pulled me, tugged at my suitcase, and we walked through the gate daring not to look back. As soon as we were out, we both ran, only stopping when we reach the bottom of the hill where the buses were waiting. We quickly jump onto the bus, and it is only when we are on our way that I looked at my mum, she looked worried and frightened. When she caught me staring at her, she half smiled reassuringly, and it is then I exhaled.

July 1991

Three years had passed and today was the last day of university. I had left home this morning like any other. However, this time as I stepped out, I knew I wasn't ever going to return. I felt nervous and frightened. I had planned my escape with precision and prayed that nothing would go wrong. Mother looked over at me. She hesitated before she spoke, sending my mind into overdrive. Did she know, had she found out? I silently prayed that she wouldn't look into my bag. She asked me to return home on time, and with that, she went back to her cleaning. I nodded, daring not to breathe, let alone look back.

Linda and I stood in awkward silence not sure what to say to each other. I looked over at her and felt immense gratitude. She was a kind lady and a good friend, someone who through travelling together to university daily brought us closer. Deep down, I knew she had been sent to me for a reason. She was going to help me execute my plan today.

Finally, she spoke; I think that is your flight Missy, you need to go. We hugged, she pulled back, I think scared that if she held on for too long, she may stop me from leaving. My mind was racing, slightly jumbled, tinged with fear. However, the thought that overshadowed all the others was the one telling me if I didn't do it now, then I would never do it.

A week had passed, and I spent my time fluctuating between keeping a low profile and remaining unnoticed, and at times having pangs of loneliness and wishing I was on a real holiday with friends. Instead, here I was all alone on a small island, thousands of miles away from home. A home that I would never see again or family for that matter. In the absence of mobile phones or keeping in contact, I could only guess. That evening when I had left, my mother would have started to panic when I didn't show up. I had asked Linda to post a letter at approximately 5.30pm, the time when I would be expected home. The letter was short and concise. I talked about leaving home to seek a life of education and career and asked them not to follow. It was best that way.

I walked through the lobby, and as I did, the receptionist called me over. I assumed, like all the previous occasions, he was going to flirt with me like he did with all the girls and seek to impress with his sultry Spanish words, which I didn't have a clue about, but nevertheless, it did sound very romantic. I smiled as I approached him. He didn't smile back. Instead, in his broken English, he said 'you know you asked me to let you know if anyone asked for you.' Well, today, we get a phone call, a man said he is your uncle. He gave your name and asked if you were here. I said no, we cannot give information. He said he was checking to make sure you were ok;' he put the phone down.'

What time did he call? Around two hours ago. Can you please call me a taxi to the airport? He nodded, daring not to ask any questions.

The seatbelt sign lit up as the aeroplane made its way to disembark. I had contacted Linda and told her that I had managed to get a flight to Gatwick. I knew that if my family knew where I was, then they would know which airport I was travelling back to, so I had changed my flight and destination in the hope that they would be thrown off the scent. Linda had managed to quickly tell me that her house was being watched and she was convinced that she was being followed.

I walked through the glass doors; my heart was racing as I scoured all the recipients watching, waiting in anticipation for their loved ones to appear. I saw Linda, she darted quickly forward, grabbing me by the elbow half-hugging half-pulling and speaking at the same time in a panic way. She had sought help from her brother who had kindly agreed to help. She said it had been hard as someone was always outside the house watching her every movement. We walked to the car park; all the time Linda nervously looking around to make sure we were not being followed.

We approached a large SUV, and the man jumped out. He had kind eyes and a warm smile. He opened the boot and apologetically asked me to jump in and placed the blankets over me.

He pushed a bottle of water in my hand. I laid still and closed my eyes as the car moved.

The next six weeks were hazy as I was moved strategically from friends and family that had agreed to help Linda in her cause to keep me safe. Eventually, I ended up as a house sitter/ lodger for Penny, whose work took her abroad and who happened to have a huge Victorian house on the outskirts, a short distance from my parents. My logic had been they would be searching the huge cities and would not suspect that I would dare set up home so close by.

I had cut my hair, was wearing English clothes, but this was not enough to disguise my identity. I leaned against the window, staring out at the unfamiliar streets and places as the bus travelled on its route. I had hardly left the house, frightened that I would be seen. I got off at the town centre. As I did, I saw someone familiar, and I recognised the smile immediately. It was my first cousin. He looked at me sheepishly as I stared at him frozen. Both of us stood, not knowing what to say. He finally spoke, you ok? I nodded. They're worried sick about you. You know that he rushed on; I think your mum is dying. You just need to get in touch with them and let them know you are ok. I nodded as I swiftly mumbled something about being late for an appointment and scurried into the crowd, only stopping when I thought it was safe to do so.

Hot tears stung my eyes. I hadn't escaped that life so that I could keep running, and this was not how it was meant to be. I half-smiled, recounting my fantasies of living in a small house by the sea, driving a car, and working. Instead, I was hiding in a city ten miles from my parents' home. I knew that as soon as my cousin had left me, he would have made contact with my family, and before nightfall, they would start searching for me. But this time, they were dangerously close.

I had tried to throw them off the scent as each week I wrote a letter, posting it to Linda's sister who lived in Blackheath, somewhere in London. The arrangement was that Linda's sister would send the enclosed envelope and post it to my parents. The stamp mark world clearly let my family know that I was living in London. But now, I had been seen close to home, the last place where they would look, but my cousin had seen me. Overwhelmed with panic and fear, I decided that enough was enough.

The café was small and discreet. The doorbell rang as I pushed the door open. Inside, there were a dozen tables, each with yellow plastic tablecloths. It was empty except for an old man who was slurping his tea in the corner. I deliberately chose a table in the middle of the café. I walked over to the counter where a middle-aged woman peered over her glasses and smiled her nicotine stained smile. What can I get you, lovey, in a thick Birmingham accent? I will take a glass of water, thank you. Little did she know this was not a mid-morning tea/coffee meeting with friends. This was meeting on which my future hung on, depending which way it went. I tried not to think or contemplate what the different outcomes would be of this meeting. I sat on the plastic chair listening to my heart beat as it got louder, so loud I swear the old man looked up to stare.

My father walked in, alone and pulled out the chair in front of me. He looked around uneasy, slightly awkward, somewhat embarrassed. He cleared his throat and said 'you look well,' then half laughed. Realising what he said, he quickly added, "why wouldn't you be? You were always smart, you should have been a boy," then he fell silent, as though deep in thought.

I realised that I hadn't thought about what I was going to say, half expecting my father to turn up with all the male members of the family who would jump me, throw a blanket over me, kid- nap me, and if I ever woke again, I would be in a faraway remote village, somewhere in the heart of Kashmir.

I spoke slowly; I didn't mean to hurt you, but it was the only way I knew. All I have ever wanted was to study, get a job, work and live my life.

He interrupted; this time, his voice tinged with anger. You could have had all that; you didn't have to run away. By doing so, you cut off my nose. The whole family, everyone, is talking about us. The shame is unbearable. I could have died very easily, but I haven't. I will never be able to gain respect from my elders, from my brothers... your poor mother is literally dying. All she does is cry day and night. The neighbours are looking after the family as best as they can. I tried hard not to let the tears roll down and gulped the lump that had a chokehold on me, making my breathing erratic.

I jumped as the doorbell rang and someone entered. Thankfully, it was a stranger who made their way to the counter. I watched him order his tea and apple pie.

Dad, I'm really sorry. I had no intention to bring shame onto the family, least of all you. I let the tears stumble. Is there a boy involved? No, I quickly replied in disgust. Offended by the sheer suggestion? No, I repeated and shook my head furiously. My dad half smiled and shook his head too; this time, his eyes glistened. I told them, I told them there is no boy. She isn't pregnant, she isn't on drugs, she's gone to seek her freedom. Then he gestured towards the door; they didn't believe me. They want to believe you have been dishonourable, they want me to disown you, they want me to take pride into my own two hands and kill you. They want you dead. If you're dead, what good will that be? You're still my daughter; it will pain me. I won't be able to live with myself. Not only will I kill you, but I will be killing myself. I nodded in agreement, daring not to breathe...

You have always been free. You have always struggled to toe the line. You are not like your brothers and sisters; you have been different, always have been. You are strong, nothing will stop you, and I'm guessing nothing will break you. I nodded, praying inwardly that this was not how it was supposed to end, where they're all going to storm in and jump. I wish I had told the lady behind the counter to call the police if anything untoward happened. Instead, here I was listening to my father give his farewell speech. This was the end.

He leaned over and placed his hand on mine. You will leave here alone. I will take care of them, and with that, he gestured towards outside. You will contact your mother regularly, and you will come and visit us, your family. You will show everyone you have nothing to be ashamed of. You will hold your head high, and you will never do anything to ever disrespect or dishonour the family name ever again. I looked at him, confused and bewildered. He patted my hand and said 'Go, leave'.

I slowly got up and walked towards the door, my heart thumping against my ribcage, the blood rushing around my head, and my face felt hot. I slowly opened the door, and the damn bell rang. I stepped out. There was no one there. I stepped out, took a deep breath, turned left and walked, then sprinted. Then I ran till I could no longer run. I only stopped to catch my breath, and as I did, the tears gushed. It was at that moment for the first time I felt free...

September 2001

I looked up at the man. He was referring to his notes when he paused and looked over at me, smiling reassuringly. I wasn't sure if he was nervous or pleased. Either way, it didn't matter. Here I was, and we both knew I would have to deal with whatever is in store. He turned to face the audience and slowly began 'As you can see, we have someone new to join us. This young lady is our new; he hesitated appointment. I would like you all to welcome Saj; Saj Akhtar, who has joined our prison this week as a Governor grade. It gives me great pleasure not only to introduce you to her, but let you know that she is the first Asian female to join the prison services as a Governor. I hope, and I am sure you will all make her feel most welcome.

I looked out to the sea of faces that continue to stare back at me. I half smiled as I slowly rose and then walked to the podium to take my place. I looked straight ahead, and it was then I slowly exhaled.

CHAPTER 1

CLARITY, CONFIDENCE AND COURAGE

IT'S BETTER TO LOOK
BACK ON LIFE AND SAY:
"I CAN'T BELIEVE I DID THAT."
THAN TO LOOK BACK AND SAY:
"I WISH I HAD DONE THAT "

WHAT GIVES A PERSON'S LIFE MEANING is unique to every individual. At one point or another, most of us find ourselves asking if we are truly living a life that is meaningful to us. In other words, are we really living the life we are meant to lead? Answering this one question involves asking many more. Are we directing our lives based on our wants, beliefs, and values? Do our choices represent the things that really matter to us? Are we the fully unique beings we were born with the potential to be? How much are our pasts still influencing who we are today?

As human beings, we are incredibly adaptive creatures. We are born completely dependent on others to care for us. And in the course of our growing up, particularly very early in our lives, we adapt to the social environments we are born into in a manner to get our basic needs met so that we can survive. We internalise impressions from our early experiences and those around us to help us to understand who we are, how to view others, and how the world works. We often take on the traits of our parents; the good as well as the bad, as if they are our own.

Throughout our development, we form adaptations to cope or deal with pain and fears. Yet these adaptations, which initially served as survival mechanisms, can later come to limit us. In addition, we often take on the value systems and beliefs of the family and culture we grew up in, or we rebel and form attitudes in opposition to these influences. Either way, it can prove difficult for us to be bold enough to develop our own personal beliefs, values, and live according to them, thereby creating meaningful and fulfilling lives for ourselves that are not purely dictated by our past.

The question becomes, how do we become the unique individual we were born with the potential to be?

How do we become our real self?

The starting point for any journey is to ask this one simple question:

Are you living your chosen life?

If you find yourself answering "no" or "don't really know" or "maybe" to this question, that is ok. It may be that while you are happy with some parts of your life, there could be parts that you do not like. Not being happy overall with your life is an indication that things are unresolved.

Should this be true, you are not alone.

Up till now, it is very possible that you have been running on the treadmill of life. A great proportion of your time has been spent on juggling, working long hours, running a home, raising your family, caring for others, days with back-to-back activities where you are too busy doing.

This, combined with not truly knowing yourself, can also result in an unfulfilling existence. Because when you do not have a clear idea about what your inner values, core beliefs, and goals are, you are likely to allow your emotions and decisions to be externally dictated. Instead of making an independent decision, you adopt the values, core beliefs, and opinions of others, most likely your parents in the first instance, peers, other influences as your own.

If you have no clear idea of who you are, you will have no clarity in what you want or seek.

Unfortunately, when you do not have clarity, you then go from situation to situation, day to day living a cycle of predictability, routine but one that does not bring fulfilment for you. Remaining in this mode means that it will be hard to "attract" the outcomes that you want because your intention is not clear enough.

You, therefore, will not expect change, and your life will accordingly not change. This often can lead to feelings of bitterness and anger, as you find yourself constantly compromising and suppressing your desires. The lens you choose to look through will be tainted by the emotions and thoughts you hold. However, the great thing is you can choose to change your emotions, thoughts, and behaviours, which will in turn change how you approach life.

The greatest and most important adventure of our lives is discovering who we really are. Yet, so many of us walk around either not really knowing or listening to our inner voice, one that shares criticisms, encourages limitations, and keeps us where we are.

Trying to understand who we are may seem like an inherently self-centred goal, but it is actually an unselfish process that is at the root of everything we do in life. In order to be the most valuable person in the world around us, the best we can be is to first know who we are, what we value, and what we have to offer.

This personal journey is one that requires breaking down - shedding layers that do not serve us in our lives and don't reflect who we really are. It also involves a tremendous act of building up - recognising that in order to transform into our true authentic higher self, we need to be open and vulnerable to our experiences. It isn't something to fear or avoid, and or rebuking ourselves along the way, but rather something to seek out with the curiosity and compassion we would have toward a new experience/friend.

Women who are constantly striving to achieve something meaningful in life crave clarity. It's the only way to reach deeper into yourself to find out what makes you come alive. We all start from somewhere confusing. Our baggage can often get in the way. However, once you define your purpose, you will become enlightened and naturally will seek to gravitate to opportunities that will take you closer to your goal.

Successful people have a definite sense of direction. They have a clear understanding of what success means to them. Everything they do is consistent with their goals. They look forward and decide where they want to be. Their day to day actions help them move closer to their vision.

Once you find your why, you will be more careful and selective about your daily actions. In the words of **Margie Darrell**, Author of *"Brave"*.

"Knowing your why is an important first step in figuring out how to achieve the goals that excite you and create a life you enjoy living (versus merely surviving!). Indeed, only when you know your 'why' will you find the courage to take risks needed to get ahead, stay motivated when the chips are down, and move your life onto an entirely new, more challenging, and more rewarding trajectory."

You have to be mindful that no single assessment is going to provide you with immediate clarity and a sense of purpose. Seeking clarity in uncertain times can be a daunting experience, and it can be very stressful if the solutions you seek don't appear when you need them. Not surprisingly, this is what 'pulls you back' to your learned comfort position and often prevents you from moving forward.

Once you have clarity of purpose, this will then challenge you to do better and commit to actions that get you closer to the one thing you really want in life. With clarity, you can pull together resources, ideas, and people for a common cause. Without it, there is wasted effort and even chaos. Clarity of purpose has the power to shape your life; your decisions, choices, and ultimately your daily actions.

I have found that Clarity is the first step to crafting the life you want. Once you are clear about what you seek and or want, then you can build a life map to take you from where you are now to where you wish to be. Clarity acts as your compass without you remaining stuck or lost, never reaching where you are truly destined to be.

When there is clarity of purpose, you know what steps to take. You are the designer of your destiny, and it's important to have a strong reason for your actions. Don't just react to what others expect of you. Sadly, for many people, years of meeting other people's expectations or desires mean that tuning into what they really want is an almost impossible task.

Many of the women I coach express the same confusion. "I don't really know what I want." Years of thinking and providing for the needs of others — partners, children, family, colleagues, clients — means that they very rarely, if ever, have they taken the time to focus and define their own wants and desires.

Exercise -Wheel of Life

One of the tools and strategies I use to help clients clarify their **'here and now'** is the 'Wheel of Life.' When life is busy, it's all too easy to find yourself reacting to situations, rather than prioritising what is important to you. Naturally, when you focus on one area of your life, that can mean another gets placed on a back burner or in some cases totally neglected. This is where the Wheel of Life (or Life Wheel) can help. It helps to provide a "helicopter view" of your life so that you can see for yourself how your life is right now.

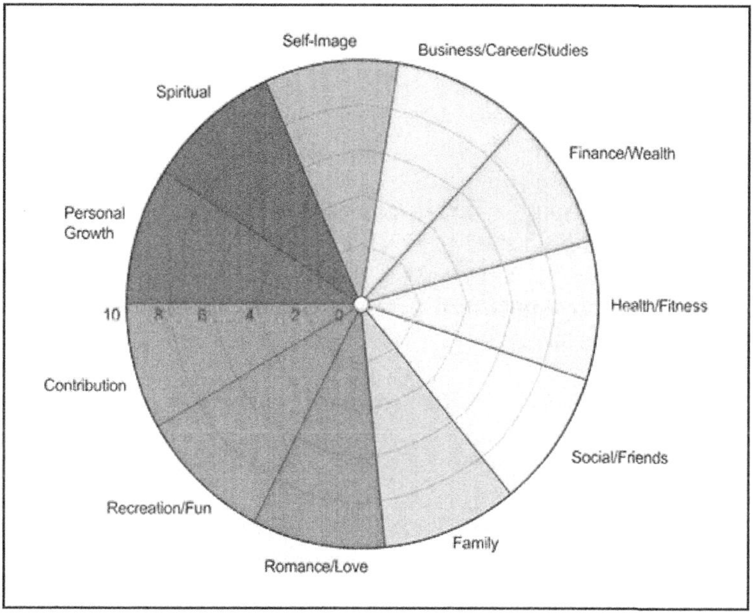

The Wheel of Life is a powerful tool because it gives you a vivid visual representation of the way your life is currently, compared with the way you'd ideally like it to be.

It is called the "Wheel of Life" because each area of your life is mapped on a circle, like the spoke of a wheel. The concept was originally created by Paul J. Meyer, founder of Success Motivation® Institute, Inc.

The Wheel of Life Exercise is a popular coaching assessment tool because it's a simple, yet powerful diagnostic tool. Although the name you give these Wheel of Life categories may vary, these areas themselves are generally the same for each of us.

The key is to determine the areas that are most important to you. However, we all tend to focus on certain areas at the expense of other areas. So your areas of focus should include both your strengths AND your weaknesses. The reason why all of the key areas are important is that many of them hit on basic human needs. And as Maslow highlights, when we don't address all of these basic needs, our lives fall out of balance.

When assessing your life, it is extremely important to be totally honest with yourself as you complete this exercise. Each section wheel represents various areas of our life.

Imagine the centre of the wheel as 0 and the outer edge as 10. Rank your level of satisfaction within each area of your life between 0-10. Then use the markings to draw a curved line in each box to visually create a wheel. (Like the image above.) Although we would all love to have a perfect 10 in all areas, that is not what it is about. The most important thing is to have balance in one's life. Even having a 10 in one area can create an imbalance in other areas of your life.

Some helpful questions for you to ask when carrying out this exercise could be:

Work/Career

- How fulfilling is your work/career right now?
- What would a fulfilling career mean to you?
- Would you say you were on a positive career path?

Money

- Do you feel financially free/financially secure?
- How satisfied are you with your current level of income?
- What impact would financial independence have on your life?

Health/Fitness

- What kind of shape are you in overall?
- If any health problems are present, are you receiving appropriate care?
- What do you do with regard to exercise?

Family

- How close are you to your immediate extended family?
- How supportive are they? Relationships
- Do you have a circle of friends that energise you?
- How content are you with your close relationships right now?
- What would make them better?

Personal growth

- Are you living the life you wanted, or the one someone else wants for you?
- Would you say you were evolving/improving?

Look at the shape of your wheel. What did you notice?

Remember that it is not about having a perfect 10 for each area of your life, but rather to have balance. The coaching wheel has many applications and is a very important part of coaching. I find it is a powerful tool to understand your here and now, offering you a true picture that can guide you to prioritise the areas you need to focus on to lead a more balanced life.

When I complete this exercise with the client, it never fails to surprise me how amazed they are that something simple can produce amazing results, i.e. a snapshot of their reality. Usually, this is followed by an immediate sense of wanting to fix each aspect of their life to make it a big fat 10. But that is not how it works. Remember, it's taken you a lifetime to carve out the life you live today. So one exercise is not going to catapult you into remedying a lifetime of habits, limited beliefs.

***

As women, I often find once we identify the problem, we are most likely to jump straight in to fix it. Remember that we are talking about you, so achieving clarity isn't the same as cleaning your house and straightening out every room. The solution doesn't lie in attacking the problem directly. If you became a kind of efficiency expert, you could probably sort your thinking out in a more orderly, focused way. But the effort would be a strain, and the results would likely be temporary. It is far better to find a way to let the mind become orderly, focused, and clear on its own.

Remember what I said earlier at the start of the book, it is important to recognise what it is that pulls us back to our position of comfort, what stops us from achieving. Once we have a clear understanding of where we are, we then can plan our next move.

The world's wisdom traditions tell us that before we embark on this journey, you need to look inside for the real obstacles that block the way to fulfilment.

It's much easier to focus on the outer demands, which consistently keep us performing daily routines that add stressors to our existence. These often only serve as distractions and avoidance of stopping and evaluating what it is that we seek.

So how can you bring vision and practicality closer together?

The important thing is that clear goals and objectives are essential to the success of any change. If you don't take the time to get really clear about exactly what it is you're trying to accomplish, then you're forever doomed to spend your life achieving the goals of those who do. In the absence of a clear direction for your life, you will either meander aimlessly or you will build a career that you don't feel good about. You may make some money, and you may do some interesting work, but the end result will not resemble anything you ever made a conscious decision to build, and ultimately, you will be left with the sinking feeling that maybe you took a wrong turn somewhere along the way.

Do you ever look at your career and think to yourself, "How on earth did I get here?"

If setting goals is so critically important, then why is it that so few people take the time to define exactly where they want to go? Part of the reason is a lack of knowledge about how to set clear goals. You can go through years of schooling and never receive any instruction on goal setting at all. A failure to understand the immense importance of establishing clear goals is also common. But those who truly know what they want often outperform everyone else by an enormous degree.

A frequent deterrent to goal setting is the fear of making a mistake.

Teddy Roosevelt once said, "In any moment of decision, the best thing you can do is the right thing, the next best thing is the wrong thing, and the worst thing you can do is nothing."

Setting virtually any goal at all is better than drifting aimlessly with no clear direction. The best way I know to guarantee failure is to avoid making clear, committed decisions.

Every day is already a mistake if you don't know where you're going. You're probably spending most of your time working to achieve other people's goals. The local fast food restaurant, TV advertisers, and the stockholders of the businesses you patronise are all very happy about that. If you don't decide what you really want, then you've decided to hand your future over to the whims of others, and that's always a mistake.

By taking hold of the reins yourself and deciding where you'd like to go, you gain a tremendous sense of control that most people never experience in their entire lives.

Many people assume that because they have a direction, they must, therefore, have goals, but this is not the case and merely creates the illusion of progress. "Making more money" and "building a business" are not goals.

A goal is a specific, clearly defined, measurable state. An example of the difference between a direction and a goal is the difference between the compass direction of the northwest and the top of the London Eye. One is merely a direction; the other is a definite location.

One critical aspect of goals is that they must be defined in binary terms. At any point in time, if I were to ask you if you had achieved your goal yet, you must be able to give me a definitive "yes" or "no" answer; "maybe" is not an option. You cannot say with absolute certainty if you've fully completed the outcome of "losing weight," but you can give me a definitive binary answer as to whether or not you are currently standing on top of the London Eye.

An example of a personal weight loss goal would be that you wish to lose 10 kg by the end of the year. That means that in order for you to remain on target, you must at least lose 1 kg per month. That is something you can calculate precisely, and at the end of the month, you can give a definitive answer as to whether or not your goal has been achieved. That is the level of clarity you need in order to form a goal that your mind can lock onto and move towards rapidly.

Being detailed and concise when setting goals is crucial. Give specific numbers, dates, and times. Make sure that each of your goals is measurable. Either you achieved it, or you didn't. Define your goals as if you already know what's going to happen.

It's been said that the best way to predict the future is to create it.

Great visions aren't hard to think up; committing to them and carrying them out is the problem! Therefore, I always insist that Goals must be in writing in the form of positivism, present-tense, personal affirmations. A goal that is not committed to writing is just a fantasy. More importantly, set goals for what you want, not for what you don't want. Your subconscious mind can lock onto a clearly defined goal only if the goal is defined in positive terms. If you put your focus on what you don't want instead of what you do, you're likely to attract exactly what it is you're trying to avoid. Phrase your goals as if they are already achieved. Instead of saying, "I will earn $100,000 this year," phrase it in the present tense: "I earn $100,000 this year."

If you phrase your goals in future terms, you are sending a message to your subconscious mind to forever keep that outcome in the future, just beyond your grasp. Avoid wishy-washy words like "probably," "should," "could," "would," "might," or "may" when forming your goals. Such words foster doubt as to whether you can really achieve what you are after. And finally, make your goals personal. You cannot set goals for other people, such as, "my personal trainer will help me to lose the weight I need to lose." Phrase it like this instead: "I am exercising daily so that I lose 10 kg by the end of the year."

Setting clear goals is not a passive act. It doesn't happen automatically. You must take direct conscious action in order to make it so. Everything counts, and nothing is neutral. You are either moving towards your goals, or you're moving away from them. If you do nothing or if you act without clarity, then you are almost certainly a victim of "being outgoaled."

In other words, you are spending your time working on other people's goals without even knowing it.

Each day you spend, working without a sense of clarity about where you're headed, is a step backwards for you. If you don't actively tend your garden, then weeds will grow automatically. Weeds don't need to be watered or fertilised. They just grow by themselves in the absence of an attentive gardener. Similarly, in the absence of conscious and directed action on your part, your work and your life will automatically become full of weeds. You don't need to do anything at all to make this happen. And when you finally get around to taking a serious look at where you are and where you want to go, the first thing you'll have to do is pull out all those weeds.

Reading this book will do absolutely nothing for you unless you turn it into some form of physical action. The best thinking, unfortunately, gives you zero results. In reality, you won't even be paid a penny for your thoughts. You can have the most creative idea in the world, but ideas themselves are utterly worthless. You only get results from the physical actions you take, never for the ideas you have. In order to get any kind of tangible results at all, you must act on an idea. You must communicate it, build it, implement it, and make it real.

If you've been running your career in an unfocused manner, just waking up each morning and seeing what happens, then it is absolutely crucial that you take the time to decide and write down exactly where it is you want to go. How much longer will you continue to climb the ladder of success, only to realise too late that it was leaning against the wrong building? Just pick a point in the future, whether it's six months from now or five years from now, and spend a few hours writing out a clear description of where you want to be at that time. I know many people who aren't sure where they want to go, so they avoid committing anything to writing in order to "keep their options open." What would happen if you pursued that attitude to its logical conclusion? If you always kept your options open and never made any firm commitments, then you'd never get promoted, start your own business, get married, have a family, move to that new home, etc., except to the degree that someone else made that decision for you.

Waiting for something to inspire you and hoping that the perfect outcome will just fall into your lap is nothing but a fantasy. Clear decision making doesn't happen passively; you actually have to physically put in the time to make it happen. If you don't have clear goals simply because you don't know what you want, then sit down and actively decide what you want. That sense of knowing what you want isn't going to just come to you in the form of divine inspiration. Clarity is a choice, not an accident or a gift. Clarity doesn't come to you — you have to go to it. Not setting goals is the same thing as deciding to be a slave to the goals of others.

Your reality will not match your vision exactly. That's not the point. The point is for your vision to allow you to make clear daily decisions that keep you moving in the direction of your goals. When a commercial airliner flies from one city to another, it is off course over 90% of the time, but it keeps measuring its progress and adjusting its heading again and again. Goal setting works the same way. Maintain a clear list of goals not because that's actually where you'll end up, but because it will give you tremendous certainty in deciding what you need to do today. When someone contacts you with an "opportunity" out of the blue, you'll know whether it's a real opportunity or a waste of time. The long view sharpens the short view.

As you begin moving towards your goals, you'll gain new knowledge along the way, and you'll have to adapt your plans as you go. You may also change your vision if you get partway there and decide it's not quite what you really want. Ill-formed goals are still far superior to no goals at all.

I was once told by someone that I should end each day by crossing it off my calendar and saying out loud,

"There goes another day of my life, never to return again."

Try this for yourself, and notice how much it sharpens your focus. When you end a day with the feeling that you would have lived it the same if you had the chance to repeat it, you gain a sense of gratitude that helps you focus on what's really important to you. When you end the day with a feeling of regret or loss, you gain the awareness to try a different approach the next day.

You'll see a measurable difference in your life on the very first day you establish clear, committed goals, even if your first few attempts aren't perfect. You'll be able to make decisions much more rapidly because you'll see how they'll either move you towards or away from your goals.

On the eve of his death, Walt Disney had a reporter crawl into bed with him so he could share his vision for Disney World, six years before its completion. When Disney World finally opened, another reporter commented to Walt's brother, Roy, "It's too bad Walt did not live to see this." Roy replied, "Walt saw it first. That's why we are seeing it now."

By deciding exactly what you want to accomplish, committing it to writing, and reviewing it on a daily basis, you bring your goals into reality with the power of your focus.

Once you have clarity of what you seek, have a clear snapshot of where you are and decide which aspect of your life you will prioritise and work on by setting clear goals to accomplish this, you then need some confidence and courage to move forward. These two elements will allow you to take the next step with relative ease.

Why is self-confidence so important? It is important because it gives you courage, self-esteem, and assertiveness. When self-confidence is present, you are not afraid to take risks and to try new things.

Self-confidence is essential for a happy and successful life and is a quality of character that most people appreciate when they see it in other people.

When you possess self-confidence, you do not allow what people think and say about you to affect you, and you don't take things too personally. This means a more peaceful life.

Nobody is born with limitless self-confidence. If someone seems to have incredible self-confidence, it's because he or she has worked on building it for years. Self-confidence is something that you learn to build up because the challenging world of business, and life in general, can deflate it.

Most people are not born with this quality of character. However, you can build it up. You can build self-confidence by changing your mindset and your attitude toward life, even if various personal experiences caused you to lose it.

Self-confident people are admired by others and inspire confidence in others. They face their fears head-on and tend to be risk takers. They know that no matter what obstacles come their way, they have the ability to get past them. Self-confident people tend to see their lives in a positive light even when things aren't going so well, and they are typically satisfied with and respect themselves.

Wouldn't it be amazing to have this kind of self-confidence, every day of the week? Guess what? You can.

> *"Low self-confidence isn't a life sentence. Self-confidence can be learned, practised, and mastered--just like any other skill. Once you master it, everything in your life will change for the better."* --Barrie Davenport

It comes down to one simple question: If you don't believe in yourself, how do you expect anybody else to?

Self-confidence, like any other skill, has to be learnt and can be mastered through practice.

Your thoughts generally allow you to make decisions, assess

situations, and make determinations about you and the world. Your brain is powerful. It works with your body to initiate and control behaviour. It also feeds you the information you take in from your environment and helps you make sense of it.

You believe what you think the majority of the time, and your thoughts influence the perceptions you hold of yourself and the world.

Your thoughts, however, can easily turn from friend to foe. In the darker times of life, your thinking can become unhelpful and very misdirected. This is because your thoughts influence what you believe, and your beliefs become reality. For example, if you think that people are rude and mean, then you will believe that the world is an unfriendly and cruel place. If you think that you are unlovable, then you will believe that no one will ever want you.

Confidence can really make the difference between success and failure. So, it's not surprising that when we struggle to do something, it's our 'lack of confidence' that often gets the blame.

Confidence can't be bottled, but the good news is... confidence can be learnt. In fact, I have been teaching people how to gain confidence for over 10 years. I encourage my clients to think of confidence as a series of steps.

Each new step is just as important as the one before. It's like building a path. I want to help you along that path. I would like to share my strategies on how to gain confidence and make the most of your life.

Think about what you have already done in your life. Even if you experienced failure and unhappiness in your life, there certainly are a few achievements. These need not be great achievements, but quite simple things, like getting good grades at school or college, promotion at work, getting your driving license, or learning to swim. Thinking about those achievements makes you realise that you have experienced success in your life, and not all is failure. This can make you feel better about yourself and about your life, and improve your self-confidence.

Focus on what you did and achieved, not on what you did not

do and did not achieve.

Why fill your mind with scenarios of failure? If you keep thinking about failure, you expect and anticipate it and attract it to you, and this further spoils your sense of self-confidence. Replace the negative movie in your mind with a movie about success. See yourself in your mind where you really want to be, living the life you really want.

If you can keep watching a movie of success in your mind, you will attract success. This process would build up your self-confidence.

Take another step toward building your self-confidence and write down a list of your achievements and success, and a look at this list often.

You might say that you have never experienced success.

You are wrong about that. You might not have experienced great success, but you surely had, even if only occasionally, experienced some kind of success. Even baking a good cake, being in good relations with your spouse or children, or going for a walk almost every day is a success.

Set small, simple goals that are within your reach and go achieve them. This will greatly boost your confidence. I am talking about really small goals, such as cleaning and arranging your wardrobe, inviting friends to your house, starting to learn swimming, or taking a day off and having fun.

These small acts will make you feel better about yourself and increase your self-confidence.

Instead of focusing on negative events and expecting the worse, make an effort to focus on the positive and expect positive results. This might not be easy if your mindset has always been negative. However, with persistence, you can change your mental habits and build a positive attitude. Make a habit of removing any negative commentary running in your mind. Be firm, and do not allow negative comments about you and about your life to run in your mind. You need to be more aware of what is going on in your mind and not allow negative comments and negative inner conversations to go on.

Courage, on the other hand, may be the single most important characteristic for changing your life. Making a change requires risk and risk is scary because when you take a risk, you may fail (of course, the other side of the coin is that only by taking risks can we truly succeed).

Courage in the process of changing your life means the willingness to "look in the mirror" and acknowledge aspects of yourself that you may not know about or may not like about yourself. Courage allows you to explore your inner world and to not run from "bad" emotions you might feel as learn about yourself. Courage enables you to reject your old life, create a new course of your life and then "boldly go where no one has gone before."

Courage also provides the commitment that you need to initiate a new life, the conviction to adhere to that new path. Courage enables you to resist your old unhealthy habits and patterns, and to make difficult choices to do what is in your best interests however uncomfortable it might initially make you feel. It is courage that enables you to let go of the familiarity and comfort of your past life and grab on to the hope that a new life will be a better one.

Courage emboldens you to embrace the values that are important to you now. It allows you to act in ways that strengthen rather than undermine your self-esteem. Courage encourages you to take ownership of your life and assume responsibility for everything you do, including your mistakes and failures, as well as achievements and successes. Finally, courage allows you to welcome and accept all of your emotions knowing that only by experiencing the full spectrum of emotions will you ever be able to fully experience the "good" ones, such as joy, excitement, fulfilment, and happiness.

Having the courage to begin the process of changing your life is much like jumping into cold water. You know it will be a shock at first. It will be uncomfortable, and you will initially regret having taken the plunge. But, after you are in the water for a short while, you begin to adapt to the coldness. What was then intimidating is now approachable. What had been unknown is now familiar. What was then painful is now invigorating.

CHAPTER 2

HEAD, HEART AND HAND

—— FEAR ——
IS NOTHING MORE THAN
AN OBSTACLE THAT STANDS
IN THE WAY OF PROGRESS.
IN OVERCOMING OUR FEARS,
WE CAN MOVE FORWARD

BEFORE WE LEAP INTO SETTING OUR GOALS, we need to understand and plan for what may get in the way of our accomplishments. There are a few reasons we could be living a life that's not reflective of our authentic selves. Maybe it's fear, a fear of what others may think, or fear of failure. Maybe it's uncertainty, or maybe we've unknowingly bought into the lie that we don't deserve the life we dream of.

As for the first, the fact is that if we change our life to fit someone else's view of what our life should be, it won't be good for us, and it probably won't benefit them either. Somehow, we have to find the strength to be our true self and stop worrying about what other people think of us.

It's been said by various wise thinkers that what others think of you is none of your business.

You don't have to drop your friends and family because they

don't agree with your dreams, but you don't have to let them define you, either.

For many of us; when we dare to dream, we end up self-talking ourselves to a point of reluctance often reminding ourselves of our own limitations. This immediately reverts our position to maintain the status quo, reluctance and resistance. The crazy thing is that if you wanted to learn to drive, you would automatically go to someone who can teach you to drive. When it comes to making life choices, we expect to hold the answers within, because we believe the best person who knows me is me. Knowing yourself and doing right by you is not the same.

Intertwined with this is the uncertainty of not knowing. Maybe we're not sure what we really want. Or maybe we know what we want to do, but we don't know how or where to start.

Sadly, sometimes what keeps us from creating the life we dream of is that we just don't think we deserve it. Maybe we're punishing ourselves for past mistakes or bad choices. Maybe we don't think we've earned it. Maybe we have been told that we're not entitled to or deserve the change to live our own authentic lives.

In my own life, I have often found myself fighting a sense of entitlement - not the idea the world owes me anything, but I have a right to be here and to pursue my dreams and desires. The thing is, until you reconcile that you do have a choice, and that you are free to create a life that enables you to live the best higher version of you, then sadly we will remain as we are.

So if we realise, or suspect, that the life we're living isn't the result of our own intentional thought, what should we do? How can we figure out what we want our lives to look like, and then start creating it?

I believe the first step is to determine if any change is needed. The fundamental question you have to ask yourself is:

Do you want to change?

Until your head and heart say yes, you will not be ready to progress. The rational, conscious mind will lead you to the decision, but it is the 'why' you are doing it that will keep you motivated, committed, and achievement.

Too often, we are quick to jump to solutions; however, I have found that until I anticipate all the things that will stop me moving forward, get in the way, or pull me back, I will not be able to plan for them let alone deal with them. Hence, when we suddenly have an aha moment, we immediately leap forward to 'immediately doing with a sense of urgency' and then crash at the first hurdle. Not surprisingly, as we return to our starting position, we tell ourselves, all the things that will offer consolation, and keep us where we need to be, not necessarily where we want or should be.

There's more to life than just making it through from one day to the next, unaware and without thought.

Too often, as women, given our complexities and experience, it is no surprise that when we do try to better ourselves, it can take umpteenth attempts before it or any progress is made.

Take, for example; it's a known fact that most women struggle with weight loss. I am no exception. Since puberty, I have been in a long-standing battle with negative body image, weight fluctuation, fuelled by endless diets, eating disorders, and unused gym memberships. I can recite every known popular diet from Atkins, Dukan, Weight Watchers, the list is endless. I have made healthy contributions to the billions earned by the Weight loss industry by investing in books, DVDs, and various products.

As long as I can remember, I have been on a Monday diet. Monday for me is a good day to start something new. It's the start of the week, and I am motivated and committed to my cause. By Tuesday, my motivation and commitment begin to falter, as I cheat with one biscuit. Once the cheat happens, I have to fall off track completely. So much that I will wait for next Monday till when I can start again.

This pattern has become a way of life. I allow the inner critic to continue to batter me until I succumb to my reality of denial, distraction, and delay. As creatures of habit, we have learnt to be and whilst we may have the best will and intention to change, the know-how, it is not until your conscious mind is supported by your 'why' the emotional driver and investment, I find you never truly accomplish your goal.

Nearly three decades later, I find myself still overweight, hating the way I look, refusing to look in the mirror, and I can't recall the last time I was in a family photograph. Until recently, I was forced to have a reality check and was stopped from referring it as 'post-baby weight,' after an embarrassing encounter with some mums when at the height of conversation, I was asked how old my baby was. It was one of those 'I wish the ground would swallow me up moments' when I found myself turning deep red and mumbling 'he is eleven'!!!

You would think this experience would have triggered the need for some urgent action. It didn't, as I continued to delay for the 'right time,' distract myself with other priorities, and use denial to draw comfort that my weight issues were not contributing to my lack of confidence, becoming insular, withdrawing from social events and spiralling my binge and starve habits into a viscous uncontrollable cycle.

Many of us continue on the rollercoaster of delay, distraction, and denial until something happens that knocks off course into a space where you have no choice but to take heed. Up until this point, I was deeply immersed in trying to recover from years of postnatal depression, battling with my demons, and trying desperately hard to manage a life, which resembled a military operation of juggling being a full-time mother and work. My only comfort and companion was food.

I believe I would have continued, until one day something happened that threw me off course and forced me to face up to my own truth.

A year ago, during one of my 'daily check-in' phone calls to my mother, I heard her say that my sister wasn't feeling too great. I asked her what was wrong and she replied 'not sure, she found a lump under her arm, went to see the doctor, who prescribed her antibiotics, which clearly are not working.' I could hear the disapproval in my mother's tone. Even though she is a regular patient of the NHS, and a veteran in various illnesses and cures, she was ignorant of why this piece of information sent alarm bells ringing in my head. Trying not to sound too alarmed and cause panic, I gently asked my mother to ask my sister to revisit the doctor and, this time, to ask to be seen by a female doctor and get a 'proper check-up,' which included a physical examination. Mother, slightly surprised at my suggestion, agreed to pass the message on.

Even I couldn't have pre-empted the events that unfolded in the following days. Sadly, it was no surprise that the follow check-up led to an urgent referral to the hospital, biopsies were taken, and a week later, I find myself sitting with my sister in consultation waiting on the results. A huge part of you wills and begs for the universe to make the outcome positive whilst there is a small part of you which does not dare to even contemplate a negative just in case it becomes reality.

Trying hard to concentrate on what the doctor was saying, I have to confess that nothing prepared me for the words that were uttered. The results showed that she had stage three breast cancer, and unfortunately for her, it was one of the aggressive and unpredictable types. All I knew was stage three wasn't good, and it could only mean one thing. I tried to focus on and follow the conversation, but the words started to fade. The room suddenly felt small, as though it was closing in, making it difficult for me to breathe. I felt my legs tremble as a sudden rush of blood sent my brain into a frenzy. The room slowly started to spin, as it did, I tried to pull myself together and then I saw her. There she was sitting, calmly listening to what was being said. I had never seen her so focused, staring intently at the doctor, daring not to move, blink, breathe, in case she missed anything. Then she looked over at me and there it was… fear, resignation as though she had just shaken her hand with death itself. Amidst her trying hard to fight the tears, she bravely mustered a half smile... and it was in that moment I was able to breathe again.

I think one of the most difficult conversations has to be telling loved ones that the 'c' word somehow had managed to penetrate into our lives. Bizarrely, even though you read about it, hear about it, and assume it is out there, happening to someone else, you never think it will happen to you. Even though statistics say that one in three of us will be affected by cancer, you still live in ignorant bliss that you luckily somehow are not that one in three.

The days that followed fused into one as we all tried to come to terms with the news. The initial shock was overtaken by feelings of numbness, mixed with disbelief, anger, moments of panic, hope returning to non-acceptance, wishing and praying that somehow you could go back in time to that moment when everything was normal. Sadly, life was never going to be normal again as mortality casts over our lives like a dark shadow, sending us all into a state of fear, hopelessness, and helplessness.

As I watched everyone fall into despair and start to crumble, I realised that this was one of those moments in life that had to be approached with vengeance and grit. The next twelve months saw endless hospital consultations, copious notes of research on causes and treatments, difficult decisions, chemotherapy, mastectomy, and finally radiotherapy.

The treatment process was chronological and smooth and soon became our focus and lifeline. Each one of us allowing ourselves to be engulfed with information, technicalities, and milestones. Such conversations were safe and easy to handle publicly. However, when alone, we were confronted with the harsh reality of death itself. Endless prayers, begging and pleading God for mercy, repentance, and to work his miracle sometimes provided the temporary comfort and hope that we sought. Time stood still. Ironically, it was time we were trying to buy.

There were some key moments in that journey that became a catalyst for the change in my own life. The first I remember is being told by the consultant that although there were many different types of cancers, unfortunately, the one my sister had been diagnosed with was one of those aggressive and unpredictable types. There was treatment; however, it was dependant on her approach and attitude. He then went on to say something that was poignant, which stuck with me. In his twenty- five years' experience of diagnosing and treating women with cancer, he found that the success of the treatment was determined by the way the women responded. He explained that there were two types of women. The first, were those women, in the main white Caucasian, who after the initial shock, etc., tended to develop a fighting spirit, which led them to facing their journey with determination and successfully overcoming the disease. However, on the other hand, there were those women, who on hearing the diagnosis understandably fell into despair, these tended to be the Asian women whose families went from diagnosis to death, missing the in-between stage altogether.

This was quite a difficult conversation to swallow as I knew this to be true. In the absence of education, awareness, and cultural differences, it is no surprise that the perception held by the Pakistani community is - cancer is untreatable and leads to death. Determined not to allow my sister to fall into the latter category, I decided that we, her family, were going to try our utmost to save her at any cost.

> *Wise folk say that you should live each day as though it's your last. We are living on borrowed time. Until I saw death up close and personal, I refused to think about mortality. I believed in forever... My sister's cancer reminded me of what if there is no tomorrow.*

My sister is renowned for being overly sensitive, very delicate, and a beautiful soul who has never wronged anything nor anyone. As a conformist, she has spent her entire life living for others. She is the one that never raises her voice, argues, always shies away from difficult conversations, and always sees the goodness in everything. This was the first adversity in her life, which she had to face and overcome.

My sister taught me the true meaning and understanding of resilience and strength.

Walking out of the consultation, we sat in the waiting area to digest the news and compose ourselves before our journey home to face her husband and children. I looked over at her, still reeling from the news, trying hard to keep it together. Not knowing what to say, I asked her if she had understood what the doctor had said and if she had any questions.

Not knowing what to expect, I was overthrown by her reaction when suddenly she reached for her head, which was covered with her hijab and with a horrified and panic realisation said, 'Oh, God, will I lose my hair?' Suppressed tears gushed down her face as she sat, holding her head. I reached out, and without thinking, I said 'yes, but you have nothing to worry about, no one will guess, cos it's covered anyway.' With that, we both broke into giggles.

Being told that you have cancer and that too one of the worst kind, I'm not sure if I would have been thinking about my hair. A week later, as my sister was being counselled and being prepared for her chemotherapy treatment, the nurse told us that most women with cancer worry more about losing their hair than death itself.

You never can truly anticipate how you will respond or overcome any challenge until you are there in that specific moment, facing it head on.

Not being a family of 'talking through our feelings,' it was no surprise, each one of us avoided talking about 'the effects of cancer, and the possible outcome, 'especially with my sister until one day I found myself asking her 'are you afraid?'

She hesitated before answering, 'sometimes, no one likes to

die, she laughed nervously, but I'm ok with it... If I have to go, I have to go. I worry more about the children, mum and dad, how they will be... after I have gone.

I am sure they will cope, but I don't want for them to go through that... they have suffered so much, seeing me like this, she reached out and touched her head, which was now absent of hair, her face pale and skeletal, tears streamed down her face.

You know what keeps me going. I shook my head, the light, I looked at her questioningly. She explained, 'When I was first diagnosed with cancer, my first thought was I thought I was going to die, I thought it would happen quickly and easily. Nothing prepared me for this. I can feel it eating away inside of me. I only said yes to the treatment for the children's sake; I didn't want to take that away, that mum didn't try. But this is hell, the injections, losing my hair, the pain, not being able to see anyone, meet anyone, trapped in a dark hole, a hole that I can't get out of. There is nothing in this hole, I can't see anything, I only can feel, the pain, the cancer eating away at me. As time has gone by, I'm still here, but I'm not really if that makes sense. I have learnt to live with this darkness. Sometimes it gets too much, I become scared and then there are times when I don't want to die... the biggest fear I have is I hate the dark and then one day, I prayed for light and this light never came and I sunk deeper and deeper, then I realised I could imagine this light, which is nearly as good as having a real light. So in my hole now right in the corner, in the distance, there is a small hole and light comes through, so when I feel everything getting too much. I look over to the light, and I know that one day, it will get closer and closer, and the darkness will be over'...

We can and must believe that even in the darkest times, our faith will always hold and support us. It calls us to believe that even behind the darkest clouds, there is something more that will bring light into our lives. Hope is in the expecting and the waiting. We can never give up even when there is no visible sign that things will be better.

Fifteen months later, we are all sitting and waiting. She walks through the door, small and frail and visibly looking like a 'cancer patient.' She searches the room as we all look on desperate for her news. She rushes over to where mother is sat and literally falls into her lap, sobbing and trembling. Both remain like that for what seems an eternity as we all look on, trying not to let our minds run like wildfire. Catching herself, she raises herself and turns around. With a weak smile and shiny eyes, she says, the results have come back all clear.' Through the shrieks of laughter, hugging, I notice that suddenly the room is full of light.

Months into the journey with my sister, I found myself making an appointment with my own doctor and sharing with her the news. I also reluctantly shared with her that I had developed a 'burning sensation in my left breast.' I laughed nervously, hinting that it probably was my way of sympathising. I tried not to let my imagination run into overdrive when after answering questions on family history, which included answers that both my grandmothers had died of cancer that I should have nothing to worry about.

Of course, an immediate referral to the hospital for a mammogram left me reeling and filling my headspace with every possible scenario, of course starting with death. I had more questions than answers.

If I was to die tomorrow, what would I leave behind, what legacy would I leave behind, how would I be remembered, what would happen to my babies, what would they have of me... how had I lived my life, had I been a good person, did I have enough points to gain entry into heaven... or had I just wasted my time? Had I done right by people, how would anyone remember me?

The next two weeks as I waited for my results, I spent my time alone, quiet, and for the first time to be still.

I was in this time of stillness, as chaos, routines, the noise subsided that I started to see my truth not with my head but with my heart.

Your heart is your centre of intuitive wisdom, and it holds many of the answers your thoughts will never provide. The head and the heart are often in conflict, but the heart never lies to you in the way that your thoughts can.

Your heart is your life force, and it works harmoniously with your whole internal system. In a more tangible way, you have noticed that the beat of your heart increases when you feel excited or anxious, and that it slows and remains consistent when you feel calm and safe.

In a more metaphorical way, your heart swells when you become open to others and life, and it closes when you experience a threat or hurt. Your heart responds to energy, so when you're around people who treat you poorly or disrespectfully, you feel yourself shrinking and becoming depleted of the organic love your heart has to offer.

Many of us stay stuck in bad relationships or tolerate being treated horribly because we rationalise the behaviour of others with our mind. We "think" our way out of situations by telling ourselves that we are being irrational or too demanding.

The heart screams to get out, but the head asks questions and looks for solutions. Your heart is a whisper, so you have to remain quiet to hear what it has to offer. Your heart cannot be controlled or influenced... it just is. Tapping into your heart is touching base with your core where the truth of your body communicates to you daily. You were trained to focus on your brain and your mind and to distrust your body.

Coming back to this heart-centred place of self-trust takes courage and effort. This doesn't mean that your heart will not misguide you at times. The heart loves by nature, so it isn't designed to look for the negative or to seek out danger. It searches for the good and the wholesome in everyone, including you. It's a balance. You don't want your thinking to override your heart, but you don't want your heart to blind you to reality.

Accessing your heart, and living from this wholesome place, is an ongoing practice throughout life. Remember that you are not divided into parts. Your mind, body, and spirit all work in sync to create your authentic self. You just have to let it all work together.

Alignment is essential if we want to discover and live our life's purpose. While physical alignment will support our body, aligning our mind with our heart is the key.

How can we tell when our mind and heart are not in alignment? We will feel it as resistance physically, mentally, emotionally, spiritually, and/or energetically.

Resistance is the gap between what our mind thinks and what our heart knows. The bigger the gap means the more out of alignment the mind is with the heart, and the more resistance there is. Resistance can show up as sabotaging behaviours like procrastination, non-action, laziness, or restlessness. It can show up emotionally or mentally as irritability, frustration, boredom, doubt, fear, confusion or uncertainty. When resistance shows up in our spiritual body, we feel stuck, held back, or the Universe puts up roadblocks by closing doors on us. There is no greater distance than that of the gap between what you know in your head and what you believe in your heart. The key is to begin to close that gap and nurture the marriage that can exist between the two, creating a beautiful balance.

I also know that whilst some of you will want to take the leap of faith, there are others who will be sceptical, have reservations, and even shy away from taking the first step. Therefore, it is helpful if we try to understand what stops most of us from achieving. What are our blockers - things that get in the way?

Until you learn what will block you, pull you back, you will not be able to overcome it and move forward.

There are a number of 'blockers' that can hold you back, which I think for most women are universal.

Fear of Finding Demons

The process of examining your life under a microscope can be pretty scary and daunting. There is the fear of discovering that there can be demons in the closet. What terrifies you is that once you embark on this journey, you will not like what you find along the way. You may discover that you are worthless. Or that you are not very likeable. Rather than put yourself in pain, you would prefer to stay unaware of these demons and pretend that everything is fine. You may have taken years to burying your demons so deep that revealing them would only open old wounds.

From young, you are also taught to appear strong: don't cry or display signs of weakness. You are warned that the consequences of appearing weak or emotional or needing help can be severe because you've observed that only those that appear strongest survive. And so, you believe that there is no place for weak souls on this planet if you want to get ahead in life.

By acknowledging who you really are, you are afraid that others may find out your truths. You fear losing your relationships. Hence, you prefer that others do not know about any signs of vulnerability or weakness that you have. It can be hard to admit that you are not all that great, you prefer to put on a **mask** rather than be your true authentic Self.

When you avoid the process of self-discovery, you are basically in denial of the **real You.** You appear to be functioning, but simmering underneath.

The question you have to ask yourself is why are you sabotaging your thoughts and beliefs?

Because you have never confronted your demons, they are still very much alive. You may not realise it, but they are probably the reasons why success has eluded you or why you have never been truly happy. Things you bury never truly go away. I have always found they have a habit of resurfacing at a time of vulnerability and uncertainty.

Lack of Self Love

You may have never been taught to love yourself, from young. How can it be possible to love and accept yourself, if you have been handed more criticisms than encouragement? So you have grown up, not really knowing who you really are or what your strengths are.

You will have gone through life internalising every criticism, put down in your life so much that it starts to shape who you are and the way you are, to the point where you begin to believe you don't matter and your life becomes about others.

You crave for social acceptance. It would seem far better to adopt traits, ideas, and behaviours of people who are popular and those whom you choose to emulate. You believe that there is nothing worthy within to find out, based on your low sense of Self.

It Is Best to Stifle Your Creativity and Dreams

You may have also been taught that it is best to stifle your dreams. "It's easier to remain real and responsible. You were told from a very young age to choose a career choice based on what would be more financially viable by the marketplace than your own personal likes and natural inclinations. Even while you have an innate talent for art, music, and design, you concluded that it is best not to develop it. Rather, you focus on getting a real job that pays real money to help you and your family live a real life. The real in this is - case is defined by others most likely close to you, who are influenced by societal, cultural, religious expectations and beliefs.

As you grow older, you have fewer and fewer dreams. After all, dreams seldom come true, you say. The dreams you once had as a child were left to die.

Too Much Noise

There are so much noise and stress in your life that there is hardly any time for self-discovery. You lead a busy lifestyle, always playing catch up and trying to catch up with your routines. You simply do not have the time to find answers that may or may not result in paying the bills for you. You would rather continue life as before. If you have been functioning so far, why rock the boat now?

The negative chatter in your head will continue to fuel a self-fulfilling prophecy that your life is absolutely fine as it is. Your head will be filled with affirmations of your current status as being one that needs to be adhered to. You dare not give up these thoughts, because if you did, then there would be space, space to fill with alternative possible positive thoughts. Thoughts that include finding love for yourself and nurturing yourself.

It should come as no surprise, if like me, once you had identified what holds you back, you suddenly feel overwhelmed, daunted at the prospect of even beginning or tackling any of these.

Despite all your reservations, you know deep down that there is no turning back; you have awakened something that has been suppressed for so long and one that you had mastered to bury deep. The fact is - now that it has emerged, it is bigger than before and you, even if you tried, can't ignore it. The best thing you can do is face it so that you can move on and live your chosen life.

However, you will need to do it with support, a holding hand otherwise at the first block as you stumble, you will fall and revert to your position of comfort and convenience.

In conclusion, the more you know yourself, the more empowered you are going to be. A clear, self-understanding results in renewed confidence, centeredness, and strength.

A great philosopher once said, "You do or you do not. There is no try."

Identifying what holds you back is the first stage. Once you have completed this, what happens next is much harder, facing up to them.

Understandably, examining your life can be discomforting and an unpleasant exercise. I know, I have been through it. However, you will be grateful for starting the process of self-discovery because rewards unfold when you know more about yourself.

You need to confront your emotional issues and weaknesses because they reveal the separation from the real You. The real You is an authentic, loving, and nurturing self. However, these negative parts add destructive layers to your Being, causing you distress and disharmony.

Negative beliefs tend to infiltrate every aspect of your life. If you have feelings of low self-worth, then you are likely to carry them in the relationships you have at home, in the office, with your friends, relatives, and loved ones.

If you find yourself coming up short, do not beat yourself up either. Instead, try to understand that you can learn how to separate the negative thoughts out by decluttering your mind, which then will lead to improving your thoughts, emotions, and behaviour. Uncovering answers will help peel off layer-by-layer the negative thoughts that have been imprinted in your mind since you were young.

These negative thoughts and beliefs have been the obstacles to your inner growth. Learn to forgive yourself. When your outer Self is aligned with your inner Being, you will feel happy and free!

"You yourself, as much as anybody in the entire universe, deserve your love and affection."
- Buddha

This process is not just about unearthing stuff that you don't wish to face about yourself. It is also about honouring your strengths and abilities. As you become more aware of what you are good at, you lessen the list on weaknesses. You will find ways to love yourself.

It is important to ask yourself what you want out of life and work towards it. Aligning with your soul purpose brings about fulfilment. Without a purpose and direction, you are going to feel like a ship going nowhere. I can assure you that if you don't go through this process of evaluation on what your purpose is, you are going to experience regret.

Exercise - Rocking Chair Test

When coaching my clients, I usually spend time getting them to participate in what I call a 'soul searching' exercise. This is really about digging deep down within and allowing yourself to imagine your life from a point in your own future, usually the place near your end.

The exercise includes you finding some quiet time and space with a pen and paper and trying to answer the following.

You are going to look back from a point in your own future: Imagine you are older, sitting quietly on your rocking chair, feeling relaxed and contented, a gentle breeze is blowing, you are enjoying the late afternoon sunshine, you're remembering the current time...

What did you achieve from this current point in your life?

What are the things you want to have done, have had, have been?

What are your regrets as you look back - are there any?

What will you be able to look back on with pride and satisfaction from that rocking chair?

Now: what do you have to do now to enjoy your thoughts in that rocking chair!?

I find this to be a really powerful exercise in terms of helping clients live by their values and head where they want to go.

Of course, there are so many things that are out of our control, and that will happen in our lives that we won't expect. But within what we can control, it can be really useful to make sure that we're doing everything we can to keep what's most important to us at the forefront, and central to everything we do.

We can strike a balance between being in the moment and pursuing the things we want the most so that we don't need to have regrets.

It can be easy to lose sight of what's most important to us, to let go of dreams, to get caught up in the everyday. To live on automatic pilot. But this exercise is helpful in bringing us back to our hearts, and to what really matters.

To know a person is to spend time with him or her. In the same manner, to build a relationship with yourself, you need to spend time getting to know more about yourself. You cannot know yourself well, if you are constantly surrounded by lots of noise, friends, and family, or if you are always preoccupied in your mind and with things to do.

You tend to connect better to your inner Being when you are more relaxed. The answers that you seek, while in a state of mental relaxation, surface more easily.

"To love oneself is the beginning of a life-long romance."
- **Oscar Wilde** (Irish Poet, Novelist, Dramatist and Critic, 1854-1900)

I also have found that a pen coupled with paper can serve as a powerful life tool. There is increasing evidence to support the notion that journaling has a positive impact on physical well-being. Get to know yourself better through the process of journaling. As you write, you are connecting to your deeper Self. Your log can provide much-needed clues about your emotions, strengths, weaknesses, and areas that you never knew about yourself. They provide an opportunity for you to heal and grow.

- **Clarify your thoughts and feelings**

Do you ever seem all jumbled up inside, unsure of what you want or feel? Taking a few minutes to jot down your thoughts and emotions (no editing!) will quickly get you in touch with your internal world.

- **Know yourself better**

By writing routinely, you will get to know what makes you feel happy and confident. You will also become clear about situations and people who are toxic to you — important information for your emotional well-being.

- **Reduce stress**

Writing about anger, sadness, and other painful emotions helps to release the intensity of these feelings. By doing so, you will feel calmer and better able to stay in the present.

- **Solve problems more effectively**

Typically, we problem solve from a left-brained, analytical perspective. But sometimes the answer can only be found by engaging right-brained creativity and intuition. Writing unlocks these other capabilities and affords the opportunity for unexpected solutions to seemingly unsolvable problems.

- **Resolve disagreements with others**

Writing about misunderstandings rather than stewing over them will help you to understand another's point of view. And you just may come up with a sensible resolution to the conflict.

In addition to all of these wonderful benefits, keeping a journal allows you to track patterns, trends, improvement, and growth over time. When current circumstances appear insurmountable, you will be able to look back on previous dilemmas that you have since resolved.

CHAPTER 3

OWN YOUR STORY

OWNING OUR STORY AND LOVING OURSELVES THROUGH THAT PROCESS IS THE BRAVEST THING THAT EVER WE'LL DO.

WE ALL HAVE PARTS OF OUR STORY that are a little more difficult to own up to than others. And, since, as humans, we are wired to avoid pain, we often end up locking those portions of our tale up in a closet somewhere, never to see the light of day again.

But, if we decide to let them out into the light, and maybe even give them a little cuddle and say, "I get you" - something quite magical occurs.

Really, what it comes down to is this: You can own your story, or your story will own you. Either way, you can't re-write the past, but you can influence the next chapter.

When you own your story, you get to write your own brave ending.

When you own your pain, it sets you free.

This means firstly being honest with YOURSELF about the reality of your life, finally and completely accepting YOUR TRUTH.

As difficult as it is, what you must remember is if you continue to deny this truth, how are you ever going to be happy?

Secondly, it means taking responsibility for your life, and how you talk to yourself, it means stopping playing the victim and blaming others for what's happened. When you do this, you can make meaning out of what happened and start to become your true self.

And thirdly, it means being honest with others about who you are and the truth of your life. This doesn't mean telling your story to the world, but starting to open up a bit to friends or family in a gentle and safe way.

Keep denying your story and stop living

Maybe all of this is too much, and you've taken a big deep breath and are holding your hands up in horror, OR perhaps you can see this as a gentle invitation to reconnect with yourself and with life. Because the truth is - you're not REALLY living now, are you?

You know how important relationships are suffering because of the barriers you've created, and you can feel the pain caused by stopping others from getting close.

Imagine instead how wonderful it would be to bring your story to the light, integrate it into your life and stop it haunting you.

Sometimes, you have to look back to move forward.

As you probably know, sometimes events from the past have a mind of their own. Memories reappear at the oddest of the times, and the more you suppress, the more they emerge. When all you want is for them to disappear, you are way more emotionally reactive than you know is good for you. And you are limited by distrust, neediness, and a stunted view of what is possible for you.

If you know your past is still haunting you today, then you need to spend some time to face it and make peace before you can truly move on. When you are truly free of the past, you then can go on and simply enjoy your life.

How do I know? From the first-hand experience. For many years, I had a very rocky relationship with my parents, filled with anger and resentment about the past. My mind screamed about the "should have's" and "ought to be's." I kept an endless list about what I deserved, but thought I had missed out on. There were periods with no communication and many arguments as we tried and failed repeatedly to find a way of meeting. Until one day, I realised that I was plagued by my past, which was so time-consuming that it was hindering me from living my here and now.

In a moment of insight, I took responsibility for my own happiness. I saw that my anger was preventing me from experiencing the ease and wellbeing that I desperately wanted, so I stopped feeding it. No more stories about what should have been, no more blaming or waiting for solutions. My identity as the wounded child disappeared, and what was revealed? Peace.

The story of what happened in my past didn't change. But what I gave power to totally changed. I stopped dwelling on the past. I stopped justifying the anger. Once I learnt to let go, I felt free and at peace. Today, my relationship with my parents is the best it has ever been.

Whilst I am mindful that some of our memories are so painful and deep that only a professional expert can help. If this applies to you, then that is fine, as the first step has to be an acknowledgement that something is not right and, therefore, you need to seek help.

However, there are those memories/experiences that don't need intensive therapy/counselling. It is those that you should focus on.

Accept what is, let go of what was, and have faith in what will be

I recently stumbled on an article by Dr Gail Brenner, a psychologist and author of *"The End of Self-Help."* She beautifully captures and articulates suffering is optional. She provides the following guide:

1. The past isn't really about the past

When you look with great clarity, you will see that there is no actual thing called the past. Everything that happens in the present - it can't be any other way. Memories of events are thoughts occurring in the present. Anger or hurt about the past is happening now. Your present moment experience in the now is what keeps the past alive.

What is amazing about this understanding is that it shows you that the way out of your suffering is always in the present. You can change your perspective - now, focus on something different - now, feel your feelings - as they are right now.

If you want to heal from the past, put your attention on your present moment experience.

2. Memories are not the problem

A memory is a thought, and a thought has no power or meaning whatsoever unless you give it power or meaning. You have many thoughts about things that happened long ago, and these thoughts cause no problems. But some thoughts are sticky. You have an emotional reaction to them, and you think them over and over. You may even have beliefs related to them; for example, "I am justified in thinking this" or "I need an apology so I can move on." This keeps them very much alive, affecting your ongoing experience.

If you want to be free of the past, ***lose interest in these sticky thoughts***. Know that it doesn't serve you to repeat them and that thinking they are justified only delays your freedom. Be prepared to take a look at the pure experience of your feelings without the layer of thinking that solidifies them.

3. "Healing" means letting go so that the thoughts and feelings don't impact you

Your goal is to neutralise the story from the past so that it loses its power over you. It becomes transparent, with no meaning and no effect. You change your relationship to your thoughts so that they don't sit like a dark cloud over you. Your goal is not to:

- Make yourself forget about the past (impossible)
- Stuff or ignore your feelings (creates other problems – addiction, depression)
- Wait for an apology or acknowledgement (postpones happiness)
- Wait for time to heal all wounds (you may need more than time)
- Wallow endlessly in your emotions (painful)
- Redo the past (you can't change what happened, but you absolutely can change your reaction to what happened)

4. The path to healing opens up once you are fed up by how the stories about the past impact you

What you focus on is what will grow. If you cultivate sadness, regret, and revenge, then they will become your reality. As an alternative, be very willing to see through these stories as much as is needed. Prepare yourself to feel differently. ***Contemplate, not defining yourself by thoughts about the past.***

5. You get a jump-start on releasing the past when you take full responsibility

Once you see that the ball is totally in your court, you have set the stage for deep letting go. Your happiness is your responsibility alone, not anyone else's. You might be very familiar with feeling like a victim. But this is a passive, disempowered position, leaving you waiting for words or actions from someone else, something you cannot control.

Taking responsibility means being open to recognising how your own internal landscape is feeding your suffering. What thoughts make you unhappy? What feelings are stuck in your body and heart? How do you make yourself suffer by recycling negative memories through your mind? Being stuck in the past means that a part of your heart is closed. ***Take responsibility for going right into those bruised and tender places.***

6. Telling stories keeps the past lodged in your mind, heart, body, and spirit

We tell ourselves all sorts of stories that bring trouble to our lives. Want to be trouble-free? Here is the medicine.

1. Notice how entranced you can be by the stories of drama and victimhood that appear in your mind.
2. Just for a moment, let yourself lose interest in these thought stories. (See that what is left is a pattern of physical sensations, maybe gripping, tension, or burning. You may never have noticed these sensations before, but they have probably been there for a long time.
3. Now notice this: You are aware, and these sensations are appearing in your awareness. They come, go, and change, but here you are: aware.
4. Take the perspective of awareness, and the sensations have the freedom to be. They aren't ignored or suppressed. You aren't so busy in the story that you don't notice them.
5. Now notice: Are you suffering? No, you are simply experiencing sensation as awareness.

This is freedom - no attention to the story, experience appearing and disappearing with ease. You: unchanging, clear, undisturbed.

7. Beliefs about healing can get in the way

Besides getting stuck in the story, you might become aware of the beliefs you hold about what needs to happen for you to let go. These are simply more thoughts that keep you distracted from the heart of the matter. Here are some possibilities:

- "I feel justified in staying stuck because I was wronged."
- "It is someone else's responsibility to make this better for me."
- "If I let go, I'm somehow approving others' bad behaviour."
- "I need an apology."
- "Life is unfair."
- "It was so bad that it's not possible for me to heal."

Your life begins now, at this very moment... and now... and now. You can always start anew. Don't feed these limiting thoughts, and you won't need them to disappear. Proceed to discover that you were never not whole, that a part of you has always been untouched by the world.

8. Relationship troubles relate to your past

Unless you see through all of it, you are a product of your past and the ideas you have formed about how relationships work. This keeps the past alive in the present. Do you fear rejection or commitment? Do you feel you need approval and attention? Do you isolate or push people away? Do you need to be on top and in control? Do you have difficulty trusting? If these tendencies cause you problems in your relationships, here is your opportunity.

Untangle your thoughts and feelings about the past, and live in freedom from them as you move forward.

9. The middle path is the intelligent path

Dwelling on what happened and leaking your feelings all over the place will keep you suffering. Hiding, indulging, or stuffing your feelings doesn't work in the long-term. Instead, bring intelligence and clarity to your direct experience. Cultivate a fire for peace and ease that serves you well.

10. Finding out who you are is the ultimate freedom

If you define yourself by your past, you will be living as a fraction of what is possible for you.

Say you think of yourself as wronged or abused or victimised. Or you see yourself as having gotten the short end of the stick.

Defining yourself by what happened doesn't help you now. It's like wearing clothes that never fit. Isn't it time to take them off?

It's easy to believe in a mistaken identity. It feels so true to think we are the result of what happened or the sum total of our thoughts and feelings. But the truest thing about you is that you are aware. Life presents a passing array of experiences - thoughts, emotions, events, people. These all arise in you but are not you.

Live as the awareness that you are - fully alive, here, not in conflict with anything. Know who you are, and the pain of the past will barely be a ripple... on the surface... of the immeasurable vastness of you.

What have you learned about healing the pain from the past that has helped you?

She describes ways to let go of past hurts is to create space in both your mind and heart.

If your heart is filled full-up with pain and hurt, how can you be open to anything new?

1. Make the decision to let it go, creating space both in your head and life

Things don't disappear on their own. You need to commit to "let it go." If you don't make this conscious choice up-front, you could end up self-sabotaging any effort to move on from this past hurt.

Making the decision to let it go also means accepting you have a choice to let it go. To stop reliving the past pain, to stop going over the details of the story in your head every time you think of the other person (after you finish step 2 below).

2. Express your pain — and your responsibility

Express the pain the hurt made you feel, whether it's directly to the other person, or through just getting it out of your system (like venting to a friend, or writing in a journal, or writing a letter you never send to the other person). Get it all out of your system at once. Doing so will also help you understand what — specifically — your hurt is about.

We don't live in a world of black and whites, even when sometimes it feels like we do. While you may not have had the same amount of responsibility for the hurt you experienced, there may have been a part of the hurt that you are also partially responsible for. What could you have done differently next time? Are you an active participant in your own life, or simply a hopeless victim? Will you let your pain become your identity? Or are you someone deeper and more complex than that?

3. Stop being the victim and blaming others

Being the victim feels good — it's like being on the winning team of you against the world. But guess what? The world largely doesn't care, so you need to get over yourself. Yes, you're special. Yes, your feelings matter. But don't confuse with "your feelings matter" to "your feelings should override all else, and nothing else matters." Your feelings are just one part of this large thing we call life, which is all interwoven and complex. And messy.

In every moment, you have that choice — to continue to feel bad about another person's actions, or to *start feeling good.* You need to *take responsibility* for your own happiness, and not put such power into the hands of another person. Why would you let the *person who hurt you* — in the past — have such power, right here, right now?

No amount of rumination of analyses has ever fixed a relationship problem. Never. Not in the entirety of the world's history. So why choose to engage in so much thought and devote so much energy to a person who you feel has wronged you?

4. Focus on the present — the here and now — and joy

Now, it's time to let go. Let go of the past, and stop reliving it. Stop telling yourself that story where the protagonist — you — is forever the victim of this other person's horrible actions. You can't undo the past; all you can do is to make today the best day of your life.

When you focus on the here and now, you have less time to think about the past. When the past memories creep into your consciousness (as they are bound to do from time to time), acknowledge them for a moment. And then bring yourself gently back into the present moment. Some people find it easier to do this with a conscious cue, such as saying to yourself, "It's alright. That was the past, and now I'm focused on my own happiness and doing."

Remember, if we crowd our brains — and lives — with hurt feelings, there's little room for anything positive. It's a choice you're making to continue to feel the hurt, rather than welcoming joy back into your life.

5. Forgive them — and yourself

We may not have to forget another person's bad behaviours, but virtually everybody deserves our forgiveness. Sometimes, we get stuck in our pain and our stubbornness, and we can't even imagine forgiveness. But forgiveness isn't saying, "I agree with what you did." Instead, it's saying, *"I don't agree* with what you did, but I forgive you anyway."

Forgiveness isn't a sign of weakness. Instead, it's simply saying, "I'm a good person. You're a good person. You did something that hurt me. But I want to move forward in my life and welcome joy back into it. I can't do that fully until I let this go."

Forgiveness is a way of tangibly letting something go. It's also a way of empathising with the other person, and trying to see things from their point of view.

And forgiving yourself may be an important part of this step as well, as sometimes, we may end up blaming ourselves for the situation or hurt. While we indeed may have had some part to play in the hurt, there's no reason you need to keep beating yourself up over it. If you can't forgive yourself, how will you be able to live in future peace and happiness?

Exercise - Owning My Story

I would strongly advise that you do this on your own, and preferably when no one is around. What is important that you allow yourself the time and space to sit and reflect on your life. Only you know how it was. To truly benefit from this exercise is to be truthful. You are not diluting nor redacting. By allowing yourself to face life as it actually was will only help towards you moving on.

When I completed this exercise, I found I went through a roller-coaster of emotions. I was left feeling sad, but liberated. Once I had poured it all out, there was no going back. Imagine squeezing all the toothpaste out of the tube. Once it is squeezed out you can't push it all back. You have to decide what will you do with it. I for one decided to make peace with my past forgive and let go.

You will need a pen, paper and some quiet time alone. Start from the beginning. It is entirely up to you how much you wish to write. I found myself jotting down whatever came into my head. It doesn't have to chronological, detailed, or perfect. After all it's your story **so own it.**

CHAPTER 4

SHEDDING YOUR BAGGAGE

LETTING GO

to move

FORWARD

"Sometimes, the past should be abandoned, yes. Life is a journey, and you can't carry everything with you. Only the usable baggage." ~Ha Jin

WHEN I LEFT HOME AND STARTED A NEW LIFE, I thought that was all that would be needed for me to go on and live a fulfilling and rewarding life of my own choice. Sadly, how mistaken I was as it took years of destructive behaviours, poor choices, difficult and often painful relationships and heartache that made me realise that I was carrying a lifetime worth of baggage. Baggage that was overwhelmingly heavy and keeping me trapped in a vicious cycle of self-destruction.

Failing expectations, constantly reminded of my wrongdoings, led me to develop poor self-esteem, negative image, and hold a distorted view of the world. For the best part of ten years, I lived and breathed like a chameleon as I desperately sought love, acceptance, and belonging.

As I struggled with my desire to cling to hurtful memories and self-defeating behaviours, it dawned on me that I was afraid to let go because it was part of my identity.

The problem wasn't that I had baggage—everyone has baggage—but that it had come to define me. I didn't know who I would be without it. At that point, it hit me: I had to dig deep, discover the person I wanted to be, and then act on it.

After I identified that I was holding on to the past because it seemed too important to let go, I discovered that letting go is harder than it sounds. Letting go of long-held beliefs isn't a one-day, one-week, or even a one-year process. However, it is possible.

As E.E. cummings accurately observed: "To be nobody-but-yourself — in a world that is doing its best, night and day, to make you everybody else — means to fight the hardest battle that any human being can fight, and never stop fighting."

The Self Under Siege, a book written by Dr Robert Firestone, Dr Lisa Firestone, in collaboration with Joyce Catlett, describes the struggle that all people face in striving to retain the sense of themselves and existential challenges.

They write that to become one's own person - to differentiate and separate oneself from these negative influences, both internal and external, involves four tasks.

The first step in the process is to identify the "critical inner voices" you experience about yourself, others, and the world around you. This critical internal commentary often represents the views of our early caretakers. It can be valuable to reflect on the messages you received from their attitudes toward you, labels you were given in the family, and what each parent actually thought about you. Often, as adults, we are still experiencing our lives through the filter of these negative points of view.

Starting to identify and challenge these critical inner voices in the first step in the process of differentiating and seeing yourself and your life through your own eyes and not through a filter based on early programming. Challenging these views involves developing perspective and answering back to these voices from a more realistic, compassionate point of view toward yourself and others.

The second step of differentiation involves identifying negative traits of your early caretakers and seeing how you may be acting these traits out in your own life. Do you find yourself acting superior and looking down on others in a manner similar to how you saw your mother behaving? Do you find yourself, in a moment of frustration, yelling words at your child that your father yelled at you? Do you find yourself withdrawing from your romantic partner in a self-protective style similar to how your father was with your mother? Or do you find yourself acting without regard for another person's boundaries in a fashion reminiscent of your mother? These are all examples of common ways that negative traits of our early caretakers manifest as part of our personality. These patterns can also hurt the people in our lives and act to push them away.

It is important to admit to ourselves the ugly truth that we have been acting out behaviours that resemble the worst of our parents, often the very traits we liked least about them. The second step in the process of differentiation involves acknowledging these destructive behaviours in yourself and then making a concerted effort to resist acting out these styles of relating.

By breaking these behavioural patterns, you are acting less like a replica of your parents and more like yourself and the person you want to be. In essence, these first two steps are breaking with your parents in the sense of needing them as parents. This does not imply not being close to your parents as people. It just means seeing them realistically and, more importantly, seeing yourself realistically, as an adult who no longer needs parents in the way you did as the dependent child you once were.

The third step in differentiation involves identifying these defences in yourself and rooting out behaviours that were once adaptive but are now limiting your life. Breaking these patterns will cause anxiety, but it's important to know that you can bear it. You may have to stop self-soothing behaviour patterns or take chances by acting in unfamiliar ways. This step essentially means saying goodbye to your child self, no longer viewing the world through a child's eyes, and seeing yourself as a competent adult, who can go after the things you want and get your needs met. It means no longer having to be self-protective, or to avoid feelings for fear they would be overwhelming. It means recognising that you are now an independent adult who has little to fear from others and who can tolerate strong emotions.

The fourth step in differentiation involves developing your own moral compass, value system, and meaning in your life. What are your real beliefs and values? Are you living according to those values and with integrity? Are you pursuing the things that light you up and really matter to you? Asking yourself these questions and answering them honestly is the beginning of this process. Do your actions match with your values? Do you admire the type of person you are?

In developing ourselves, it is important to look for role models, people we admire. We can emulate and take on the traits we admire in others as our own. People we encounter and respect can help us identify the behaviour we want to adopt. This does not mean giving up our selves and becoming another person. It is simply a part of developing ourselves and evolving into the person we want to be.

Pursuing the activities, people, and lifestyles that light us up, that make us feel more in touch with ourselves, is another aspect of this process. Having transcendent goals beyond our own limited self-interest creates a sense of meaning in our lives. Kindness, generosity, and compassion toward others are fundamental for creating a meaningful life. When we act on these principles, allowing our actions to be guided by them, we feel good about ourselves and fulfilled in our lives.

Undertaking the project of differentiation of self takes a concerted effort, and it is a continually evolving process that can be arduous at times. But what other endeavours could be as valuable and worthwhile, both for yourself and for those you love?

Becoming more fully the unique individual you have the potential to be is worth the effort. When we engage in this process, we can begin to live our lives as opposed to reliving the lives of others or living out prescriptions of others. Most importantly, we can lead a life that is genuinely and uniquely meaningful to us.

Exercise - Letter For Letting Go

If you have made the choice that you want to let go of this negativity, then there are some positive ways of doing this. I've used this method myself, and it is something I support my clients with on a regular basis towards letting go.

Take some quiet time out where you won't be disturbed and get out your notepad or a sheet of paper. You are going to write a letter to either a person/people or to yourself. Your own experiences will help you define where you need to direct your energy in this exercise.

If you feel you can't find your focus for this exercise, then persevere as I know the positive impact it can have.

1. If you are writing the letter to another person/people, then this is a chance for you to write whatever you want, get everything off your chest. You won't be sending this letter, so take this opportunity to find your closure on a past experience, relationship, etc.; it may be your opportunity to say goodbye to someone... Or
2. For you, it might be that the letter that needs to be written is to yourself. You might need to write a general letter, expressing how you are feeling and that it is time to let those past feelings go, acknowledging that we need to forgive ourselves can be helpful.

The important thing about this exercise is that you are taking all of those negative thoughts and feelings out of your mind and releasing them onto paper.

Once you have written your letter and feel satisfied that you have put everything out of your head onto the paper, then it's time to let go.

There are a variety of methods for letting go; you can burn the letter, shred it, or feel the satisfaction of physically ripping it up into small pieces. The choice is yours...

You may feel emotional, you may have tears, and that's just fine; tears are good, it's all part of the healing process. Everyone is different, and everyone will react differently.

Or alternatively, you can write an honest list of the thoughts, beliefs, and behaviours that weigh you down. Grab a pen and notebook, find a quiet space, and spend thirty to forty minutes thinking and writing. It is important to be honest and write down whatever comes to mind. Don't judge what comes up, just take note.

Reflect on each item and identify the source of the thought/belief.

Travel back in time and see where you picked up these items of baggage. Do you fear intimacy because a partner cheated on you? Do you dread holidays because your parents drank too much? Acknowledge the painful memories, but don't wallow in them. Write it down and move on to the next step.

Find at least one positive in each hurtful experience/situation.

Look for the silver lining in your cloud. For example, my mother's criticism made me aware of the power of words and taught me the importance of speaking with kindness. Looking for the good in the past helps you reclaim your power. You are no longer a victim; you decide what you take from that experience.

Create affirmations to foster change and counteract negative thoughts.

Take the positives from step four and turn them into affirmations or statements of intent: i.e., "I will speak with love" or "I will treat people with kindness." This emphasises positive future behaviour and frees you from the past. Make the affirmations tangible: put a reminder on your phone, write them on post-its, or put a list on the fridge.

Practice patience and mindfulness.

It takes time to change habits, especially when they are rooted in deep hurts or fears. Check in with yourself regularly using journaling or meditation. If you find yourself shouldering old baggage, be sure to acknowledge it, then gently release it and focus on your affirmations. Replacing negative thoughts with positive actions will help you let go for good.

There are infinite possibilities for each of us, baggage notwithstanding. Everyone has pain. It's part of what makes us who we are. What defines us, however, is how we handle it.

By taking the time to identify and understand our baggage and making a conscious decision to let go, we free ourselves to experience life in a richer, deeper, more meaningful way.

CHAPTER 5

EMBRACING THE NEW YOU

TODAY I CLOSE THE DOOR TO THE PAST, OPEN THE DOOR TO THE FUTURE, TAKE A DEEP BREATH AND, STEP ON THROUGH AND START A NEW CHAPTER IN MY LIFE

CHANGING YOUR LIFE in any significant way is difficult.

The leap of faith involves having a basic belief in yourself and a fundamental trust in the vision of who, what, and where you want to be in the future. The leap of faith involves your commitment to creating a healthy, new life and the belief that good things will happen when you do make that change.

I also know that there are many young girls and women like me around the world who, for whatever reason, have not been able to live their chosen life. A life of their own making and choice. A life where there is fulfilment, and joy.

From a young age, we are often taught, in both subtle and overt ways, to compromise who we are and to replace our true thoughts and feelings with false masks. We do this because we want to be accepted, to fit in, and to be loved, and we fear that our true self may not be good enough. Over time, our awareness of our authentic self slowly recedes. Yet, compromising our truth brings no true reward. Not knowing and loving our authentic self creates loneliness and cuts us off from our centre of power and inner joy.

The journey of discovering your true self promises to be the most rewarding experience of your life. You did not come into this world to be a prisoner to societal pressures and the expectations of others. You are here to set your spirit free and to know, express, and love all of who you are. Yet, knowing our truth is both simple and impossible.

Despite the many influences that seek to confine you to complacency and suppress your inner truth, the journey of discovering your authentic self is natural and always unfolding. The process of becoming more aware of and being in sync with your constantly evolving authentic self tends to unfold in three phases: awareness, transformation, and awakening.

Awareness

Awareness is the ability to be attuned to the present moment and the deeper calling of your spirit. We have come to know ourselves through such things as our race and gender, our socioeconomic circumstances, and societal norms. Throughout our lives, we receive many well intended, but soul-suffocating messages to quiet our authentic voice and comply with the expectations of others and the values of our environment. Some of the personal characteristics, qualities, and likes and dislikes that we unknowingly adopt to fit it may reflect our authentic self, but others may not.

To discover what is true for you, take a look at yourself and the world around you. Listen to and trust your intuitive gut feelings and allow your heart to guide you. For example: Examine how you spend your time and what you put your energy into. Is it reflective of your inner truth? Does your current job or career provide you with a sense of purpose and meaning? What is the quality of your relationships? Can you express your innermost feelings and thoughts to the people in your life? Do you have an interest that you would like to explore or is there something that you would like to be doing, but you fear that others may not understand or reject or laugh at you?

Allow your true thoughts and feelings about your day-to-day responsibilities, patterns, and activities to surface. You may at times unknowingly compromise and limit yourself out of habit. From a young age, you may have suppressed your true desires, aspirations, and dreams and do not realise that you are continuing to do this.

Transformation

As you listen to your intuition and allow your thoughts and feelings to surface, false layers of self begin to fall away. Transformation and change come your way as you consciously let go of what no longer speaks to your true self. For instance, you may become aware that the job that you have held for many years is no longer satisfying. You are ready to take the leap and go back to school and pursue a much-desired career path that you previously did not think was possible.

Sometimes change is sudden and unexpected. A much-longed for opportunity comes your way with little effort on your part. Your boyfriend or girlfriend ends the relationship, or you are laid off from your job. Sometimes change is more subtle. You are able to trust others and open your heart as well as share and receive love and connectedness at a more intimate level. Perhaps you feel disconnected from those things and activities that once brought you a sense of belonging and joy. Maybe you feel an inner void or a soul longing, but you do not know why or how to heal it.

Transformation can bring a sense of inner relief as emotional expectations and burdens drop away, or it can be more challenging. As we shed false beliefs, things, and activities, our sense of security and our connection to others may falter and diminish. Yet, letting go is part of the cycle of soul growth and ultimately leads to the authentic awareness of self. When we submit and allow change to happen and become more comfortable with insecurity, new energy and possibilities begin to emerge.

Awakening

Transformation ushers out the false aspects of self and invites you to know yourself in new ways. Similar to transformation, awakening can be a gentle unfolding of new awareness or the sudden realisation of truth. For instance, through a deeper alignment with your authentic self, you may become more aware of those actives and practices that help you to feel more peace and joy in life. When you let go of the expectations of others, you find the courage to choose what feels right for you even if there is a lack of support from family and friends. Others' opinions and judgments no longer control your behaviour and sense of self. More independent and able to do it alone if necessary, you feel positive and enthusiastic about the future.

Sometimes awakening can be more challenging. For instance, you may realise that you have to confront a truth about yourself that you have denied. Maybe you have given your power away to another out of fear of being abandoned or being alone. You may awaken to the reality that you are in an unsatisfying or controlling relationship and that you and your partner need to work toward positive change. Maybe you have an interest in a type of spirituality or practice that you have kept hidden from others because you fear that they would not understand and accept you.

Yet, despite how disruptive, surprising, or confusing change may be, awakening always leads you deeper into the core of your authentic self where your true power and joy resides. With awakening comes an increased sensitivity to the world around you and a new appreciation of your own heart-centred depth and inner truth. You become aware that what is inside of you is more powerful than what is outside of you. The loud voice of the world's standards and expectations subside as your intuition strengthens and you trust and act on your what is right for you.

The process of awareness, transformation, and awakening has no true end. On the journey to discovering your authentic self, you are constantly cycling in and out of these phases. As you awaken to new aspects of your core truth, you are transforming and becoming aware of others.

How you transition into the next stage will wholly depend on you - as the person you are. I'm a huge believer in a simple concept that can change your life: Who you have been is not who you have to be.

At the same time, who you are today will determine who you are in the future. The way you live your life today determines the quality and experience of your life tomorrow.

As independent, self-aware women, we get to decide who we want to be, every single day. And who we are is a function of what we do, so whether we are consciously trying or not, we are always crafting our future self.

But are you crafting your *ideal self?* How conscious are you of the self you're creating right now? Put simply: Are you in the process, every day, of becoming the woman you want to be?

Deciding who you want to be, matters.

Every day, we make choices — some big, some small. Those choices add up to who we are today, and who we will likely be tomorrow. Whether it's what you're having for lunch or what you say to a frustrating colleague, you have (literally) hundreds of chances every day to define who you are.

Without that conscious direction, your identity is left to forces, patterns, and stimuli beyond your control. The job you stumbled into, the personal history of loss or disappointment, even the apartment or the neighbourhood or the movies you watch

— these will all, by default, determine who you are, if you don't consciously decide to choose them for yourself.

The phenomenon of waking up one day to discover that you're living a life you don't truly love is a real one. It happens when you don't actively decide who you want to be. Without a captain at the wheel, a ship will just capitulate to the sea. So will your life. If you want to become a better person, a more fulfilled person, you need to take action.

The "trick," if we can call it that, is to be aware of every choice you make, and use it to build yourself into the woman you want to become. Because some of our decisions can move us toward who we want to be, while other decisions can move us *away* from that person. The good news is, when you view every decision as a building block, you know the next decision about who you want to be is just around the corner. We are creating ourselves at every step.

It can be intimidating to realise that every decision contributes to the woman you want to be. If you want to become a better person, though, you must constantly bear this in mind. I understand being daunted at first. But there's something very powerful about radically taking responsibility for your life. When you accept that only you can make decisions to become a better person and build yourself into the kind of woman you want to be, you give yourself an enormous amount of power.

Compare this mindset with the default one, in which you view yourself as largely created by external forces. That worldview can be easier — at least it can feel easier — but it's also far less secure, fun, and empowering. Our real power as individuals comes in how we choose to react to those forces. If you lose a job you love, for example, you have a few options. You can choose to stew about it for a week — that can feel very satisfying, natural, and easy. Or you can acknowledge the loss and choose to throw your negative energy into finding an even better job. Or you can sit with the feeling as you go on a five-mile run, contemplating your next move.

Either way, your choice is determining the person you are *now.*

And we're not just talking about chasing big dreams. This isn't about turning around from a loss and then, say, deciding to run for Prime Minister. This is about recognising that however you respond to your life situation — big or small — you are determining the quality of your life tomorrow. Wallow in self-pity, or go for that run. Stew in the disappointment, or take a risk by applying for the job you've wanted all along. The possibilities are only limited by our own imagination. "Reasonable" is a lot more ambitious than you think.

Exercise - The Future Self

YOUR FUTURE SELF IS WATCHING YOU RIGHT NOW THROUGH MEMORIES.

If you knew you had access to a source of wisdom that would always lead you to make the most effective and right decisions in your life and business, how empowered, how confident do you think you would feel? How could this knowing give you a sense of faith and comfort that could move you past any stumbling blocks or issues that may be keeping you down.

As a professional coach, one of the techniques I utilize with my clients to give them clarity about their choices and direction is through the visualization and connection with their future self. The future self is an imagining of yourself, let's say several years down the road that is unfettered by doubt, fear or negative conditioning from the past. The future self takes you beyond self-imposed limits and is in alignment with your core values, and what it takes for you to truly be fulfilled and successful.

The future self

If is your highest and best self which knows what is right and true for you in every situation. It has a way of sorting out and prioritizing the most meaningful and important issues in your life, and it is not particularly interested in pleasing others, tolerating or settling. The future self illuminates a path for you to follow and embody. It is one of the most powerful exercises that I have had the privilege of using in working with my clients.

Becoming Your Future Self

Let me point to a specific example of how working with the future self can empower someone to make positive changes. Not long ago I facilitated the process with a client. After leading her into a calm and relaxing state, she was able to vividly describe her future self 10 years from now. She saw this woman living in a comfortable home in another part of the country with a new occupation as a writer and motivational speaker. She also described her future self as glowing with an inner radiance, contented and sure of her purpose.

One of my promptings during the exercise was to have my client ask her future self what beliefs she needed to adopt, and what steps she needed to take to get from where she is now to where her future self is 10 years from now. We have used that question and other inquiries to shape her current plan and actions. She has stepped out of her current box and is now learning and trying new things that are in alignment with the aspirations, values and accomplishments of her future self.

As her coach, I am challenging and motivating her to step into the shoes of her future self. If a fear or doubt creeps in, we address it, and I remind her of the powerful self she is moving towards. Through the eyes and perspective of her future self, the issue that bothered her does not seem as important or taxing.

Alternatively, a great place to begin is to think about the men and women that you admire. So turn off your computer and phone, sit down with a piece of paper and a pen and then make a list of those people that you admire most. You can pick anyone from your mother to Oprah Winfrey to Bill Gates to Mark Zuckerberg. It's one of those questions that doesn't have a "wrong" answer. After you have a fairly extensive list, pick five who really stand out for you.

Now ask yourself and note

Why do you admire them so much? What qualities of theirs do you want to emulate? Then go further: Ask yourself why *you* admire these qualities. For example, maybe you admire Oprah Winfrey because she reached the heights of success against all odds. Great. But why? Is it because of her dedication, resilience, her ability to interact, impact, and influence others and help change lives or the fact that she never gave up in the face of adversity nor lost her self-belief?

Don't be afraid to be brutally honest. If you answer what you think the "right" answer is, you'll miss the beauty of this exercise. Get to the heart of why these individuals speak to you. In the process, you'll discover their own motivation and reward for becoming the individuals they are.

Combine this with defining and setting your goals can navigate you towards the direction you need to be in — and really *should be* — one of the most pleasurable activities you can engage in. There's something about the process of dreaming about the life you want — coupled with the electric tension of what you need to do to get there — that's always really excited me.

So fill up an entire page with what you want your life to be like. Don't censor yourself. You will be amazed at how many of your "unreasonable" goals are totally attainable.

Then, think about why you want to achieve these goals. For example, you might think you want to be rich, when in fact what you really want is lots of free time (which sometimes doesn't require money at all). Or perhaps you want prestige, or recognition, or something else that money really can't buy. Digging a bit deeper into the why of your list gives you a more nuanced understanding of your goals. You'll probably find that at least one of your goals is just a means to some other end.

At the end of this exercise, you'll have a list of goals you'd like to achieve, along with a more profound understanding of why these goals actually speak to you.

Once you have heroes, goals, and motivations, you've got a much clearer idea of what kind of woman you want to be. Now you need an action plan for personal growth and change.

To that end, make another list — your final one. Formulate a daily routine to help you move toward your goals. No matter what they are, articulate what you want to do every single day to move forward. Whether it's writing a page in your novel, going to the gym, or spending an hour a day growing your side gig, work toward your goals every day.

Again — those tiny decisions today determine your tomorrow. Translate your goals into a set of habits and practices, and the abstract concept of who you want to be will start to take on a day-to-day reality.

Along the way, document your progress toward becoming the future you and learn to appreciate your journey.

Take ten minutes every night to look back on your day. How did you live up to your goals? Are you honouring the qualities of your role models? Did you achieve the actions you set out to do at the beginning of the day?

As I previously said, journaling is a great way to keep your eyes on the prize. Perhaps most importantly, it offers the opportunity to praise yourself on a regular basis for the work you're doing. When you've turned what it takes to be the woman you want to be into a series of daily tasks, it can be easy to lose sight of progress you're making.

Use your journal to acknowledge that. If it feels right, go ahead and identify opportunities where you could have *realistically* made more out of your day — but don't beat yourself up for not being Superwoman. Being honest and recognising your progress is a powerful way to boost your self-awareness and your self-esteem.

Finally, remember that this journey is ongoing. It never truly ends. If how you spend today determines your tomorrow, then tomorrow determines who you'll be the following day — and that person might experience real personal growth and change, often in profound and dramatic ways.

And remember, don't avoid or lose sight of your own evolution. The point of analysing your role models, setting goals and developing an action plan isn't to fight your way to completion. There's no "end game" in your personal development. The idea that you grow up to a point and then stop is a myth. What we're talking about here is an open-loop, always-evolving journey toward becoming a happy, healthy, effective person.

So that's the final piece of this puzzle. In order to experience real personal growth and change, and to become the woman you want to be, embrace the fact that you will *always* be in the process of becoming that woman. It's up to you to join that journey and stick with it. It begins by recognising that you can grow into the person you want to be. And it continues by always reflecting on who that person is.

CHAPTER 6

NEW BEGINNINGS

YOU
CAN'T START
THE NEXT CHAPTER
OF YOUR LIFE
IF YOU KEEP RE-READING
THE LAST ONE.

IT ONLY SEEMS FITTING TO SHARE WITH YOU how I came to be here, writing this book, sharing with you my story.

Along with supporting my sister on her journey of fighting and beating cancer, something profound and if not more traumatic also happened affecting my professional life.

14 June 2017

Like the millions around the world, I woke up to the images that flooded through onto the television screen showing a high rise Tower in West London on fire. I have to confess, immersed in my morning routine of breakfast, preparing packed lunches, and looking for missing bits of uniforms, I didn't pay heed to the details. Occasionally, I looked up, to see images of women, children sat around in their nightwear, clearly distressed from the events that had taken place.

Having battled through the morning rush hour, then jumping onto the train, I finally reached my destination to a busy morning of meetings. It was around lunchtime when I was standing in the office and happened to look out of the window. There in the distance, I saw the dark smoke rising from a charred building spiralling high into the sky. I swung around to hear colleagues discussing the fire and how sadly news was trickling in that there were fatalities, total number yet unknown. In the following afforded moments, I felt saddened by the tragedy and prayed that the fatalities were few, as I rushed into my next meeting.

Days later, an email popped up in my inbox, inviting expressions of interest from those who wished to help the victims of Grenfell Tower fire. The roles were unspecified, and the expectation was to start imminently.

Not entirely sure why, I submitted an application.

A week later, I stepped off the tube at Latimer station. Never having been to these parts of London before, I wasn't sure what I had expected.

In the absence of any induction, settling period, the instructions were clear that all of us who had joined the team were expected to hit the ground running and try to help a whole community who had been displaced, traumatised, and suffering immense grief.

An eerie emptiness hit me, like the aftermath of a war zone often seen on TV. As I followed the road to where the tower was, I saw street railings were lined with flowers, pictures of loved ones still missing with pleas of messages, small teddies, cards...

I slowly walked, only occasionally stopping to read the personal messages. I couldn't bear to stare at the images of smiling, once full of life photographs.

My stomach churned as I tried to fight back the tears as the enormity of what had taken place hit me as I found myself face to face with the Grenfell tower... It stood tall, burnt, hollow like an open coffin, representing death where once life had existed.

In that stillness, I found myself hearing the cries, screaming of those who desperately tried to escape, and those who desperately tried to help, watch on unable to do anything to help.

I have chosen not to divulge the details of my work with the Grenfell community, out of respect for the ongoing work.

However what I can share, I had never been up close and personal to trauma, death, and loss in the way I did with this community. My own life took a back burner as I and many like me tried to help this community to come to terms with what had happened. As cliched as it sounds, time does not necessarily heal, it does however, allow us to deal with pain and the void left behind after losing a loved one.

My days, evenings, weekends fuse into one. I lost sight of my own family as I tirelessly and relentlessly tried to do everything I could do to help. It no longer was 'a job,' it became a 'way of life. I hadn't appreciated the impact it had until some six months later.

It was Christmas Eve, late evening, tired I placed my key into the door to let myself in. I hesitated as suddenly I felt overwhelmed with a feeling that I didn't recognise. For the first time ever, I didn't wish to go inside my own home where I know both my babies would be waiting.

It always makes me smile, on cue as soon as the key is turned, my little ones, no matter where they are in the house, leap into action and rush to the door. Immediately jumping onto me with screams of laughter and joy the word mummmmmmmmmy... extended, the hugs tight. Time stands still, and everything disappears.

This evening, I didn't wish to enter. My hands trembled as I deliberately turn the key, so quietly as to not alert anyone in the house. I could hear the television in the lounge. I dropped my bag, and it was here that I sat in an inconsolable mess.

Moments that followed were filled with faces, echoes, stories; everything that had gathered over the past months came to the forefront. I felt this immense guilt of coming home to my own family when I knew there were those that would never be able to go home, never be able to hug their loved ones, never be able to feel and live their lives with their loved ones. And I knew that as Christmas day dawned, there would be many wishing and praying for this day to be over...

I'm not sure how long I lay crumpled on the stairs in a heap before my husband found me. For the first time ever, his arms around me did not provide any comfort.

Another six months passed before I decided that it was time for me to leave my role with the Grenfell community. It was a difficult decision, but one that I recognised that needed to be taken. Although the work in rebuilding the community had only begun, I accepted that I had gone as far as I could on the journey and 'it felt' right to exit.

As my supporting role to my sister and the Grenfell community started to diminish, I found myself in a huge vacuum of void. For the first time in a long time, I felt lost and unsure. Now having time on my hands as I started to reconnect with my 'old life,' I found myself asking questions and reflecting on what it was that I would be returning to.

It made me realise that I had spent the best part of two decades, drifting, going from situation to situation, job to job, relationship to relationship not fully appreciating that whilst I had managed to break free from the life I had been born into, I had recreated a similar world where, this time, I was my own constraint, foolishly believing if I fulfilled wishes and expectation of others I may just find happiness and contentment.

The realisation was compounded by not knowing how long I had remaining, here in this one life. I knew that somehow, I had lost my way. I had trundled from job to job, making ends meet constantly feeling stressed, running on reserves.

Someone once said death always comes unannounced and adversity hits you when you least expect it.

It was during this space that I asked that heavily loaded and most dreaded question that we can often spend a lifetime trying to answer.

What is my purpose?

There is an awful lot of literature out there on how you can discover your purpose, what it means.

For me, however, I found what I was looking for by looking deep within.

We cannot thrive until we discover it, and we cannot fail to thrive as long as we align ourselves with it every day. Everyone has one, and each person is different.

You may think a lot, even worry a lot, about what you "should" do with your life. Should you keep your job safe or leave it to follow your bliss? Should you have a baby now or party hard? Should you make lots of money while you can or travel the world? Should you start a non-profit organisation or change the system from inside it? It's easy to trip out on questions like these, but they are the wrong questions to be asking if you want to thrive.

Your purpose has nothing to do with what you should do (or not). It is not about being right or wrong. It has nothing to do with what your parents think. It has nothing to do with being rich, respected, or famous. It's not even about what you want or desire.

Instead, your life purpose emanates clearly from your body/mind once it is free from patterns. It is your truth once you have reached peace within.

Purpose is the way you can be each and every moment of each and every day that brings the most of your potential into the world. It is the glue that connects your brilliance with what your community needs most. It is a bridge between your unique gifts and what the world wants most from you. You can't second-guess it with your head or force it to be something it isn't with your hands. It may not be convenient, moneymaking, or safe. Many of your loved ones may not understand it. Some may resist it. Yet, it does not matter who thinks what about it. It is your truth.

To find your life purpose, first, you have to let go of all the patterns that have gotten in its way for years.

This doesn't mean that, once you discover your life purpose, you will have life all neatly sorted out on an Excel spreadsheet. Far from it. Purpose constantly evolves. You can't control it. You can't plan in detail how it's going to work out. You just have to feel it and allow it to emerge from you, free from patterns.

Purpose is who you are when you are free from being protective, fearful, or aggressive. It is the future pulling you into it, uniquely shaped by the experiences in your past.

If all our old patterns are enshrined in stories that limit us, hooking us into blame, shame, and complaint, our life purpose is a new story that opens up a world of possibility to us. The more of the old story we give up, the more of the new story we reveal. We have no idea how the story will play out, just that we are enacting it at the moment in constant interplay. By getting into the conversation that is purpose, we start to weave a tale that makes sense of the things that have happened to us; and how they can be meaningful for the problems we (and usually other people too) are having today.

No one can tell you that the new story you are weaving is "right" or "wrong," least of all your parents or friends. That doesn't mean to say that they can't challenge you or give you useful feedback when you are off track, off purpose. But it does mean that it is always your choice how to make sense out of all your experiences, both painful and pleasant, so you can focus your attention meaningfully on the here and now. Only you can weave the story in which you are playing the lead role.

If you can't tell an inspiring story about where you've come from and where you're going to, nobody else will do it for you.

Our life purpose is always as much about the world—the people we love and the communities we live in—as it is about us.

Our happiness is massively dependent on how we connect with, and contribute, to others. In a survey of 200,000 adults across 136 nations, people who gave to others were the happiest. That was true whether they lived in rich countries or impoverished ones. When we care, we get a boost to our happiness levels equivalent to someone doubling our income overnight. Being of service to others can even extend life expectancy and boost health! Caring for others can be more important than having self-esteem when it comes to our own success. Being self-centred also costs us a lot of energy, as we have to keep fighting our natural desire to contribute, which kicks us out of flow.

However, we must find a balance between giving to others and nourishing ourselves. Purpose needs to be grounded in our wellbeing as well as that of others. We have to keep rooted and resourced.

Finally, Purpose isn't a career choice, brand vision, or goal. It is how you care and share at any time, with anyone.

When you let go of all the "shoulds," you will almost certainly discover that your purpose amplifies one of: playing, experimenting, creating, learning, sharing, loving, caring, teaching, transforming, adventuring, or healing. These are all ways to contribute to the flourishing of others while blossoming yourself.

Free from doubts and fears, cynicism and self-criticism, your life purpose is the sum total of every bit of love and wisdom you have gleaned from your life experiences, mixed with the skills and talents that you have honed through engaging with them wholeheartedly. Your life purpose is who you are when you feel most alive, most of use, most awake.

You don't get to choose your life purpose. It is the result of the unfathomably complex interplay between genes, experiences, upbringing, and environment. But you do get to choose what you do with it.

You don't have to share your purpose with anyone. But if you do, it's not unusual to share it with passion and conviction, only to find the people around you responding to your beaming face with looks of disbelief or downright fear. Our loved ones may not get it at first. In reality, they may never get it. People who haven't found their life purpose, and who don't feel deeply connected to themselves, are often challenged by those who live purposefully. It can freak them out. Change can be extremely threatening, so it's important to empathise with your loved ones and allow them time to adjust to your higher frequency lifestyle. It may take a while.

Whether people around you get it or not, they are not you, and you cannot live your life for them (and they can't live theirs through you). This doesn't mean being selfish or ignoring your duties. It means finding how to join up all the competing needs in your life within a purpose story that comes from your truth, from your connection to nothing else.

We thought that we had the answers, it was the questions we had wrong."—Bono

Exercise - Finding Your Purpose

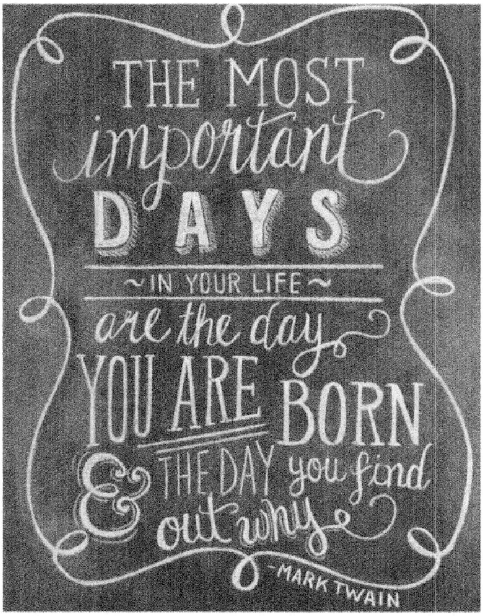

The purpose of your life is to discover who you are. It is to meet yourself and to identify what you are made of and what you are made for. To do this, you have to be willing to give yourself some special attention. You have to stop "going" "doing" and "chasing" and start spending more time "being" with yourself. You have to connect consciously with what I call your unconditioned self, the original essence of who you are. Your unconditioned self wants you to know yourself. It wants you to know who you really are.

Exercise: Book a meeting with yourself, and explore this question, "From 0 to 10, how alive do I feel?" Zero represents "the living dead," and 10 represents "100 percent alive."

Notice how alive you feel in your life right now, and identify what would help you to feel even more alive.

In particular, name specifically what inspires you and what motivates you to show up in your life each day. To live your purpose, you have to dare to be even more of who you really are.

Finally.......

If you have read this book and reached this stage where you are contemplating what to do next, you have two choices.

One is to shelf this with all the other books and return to your life as you know it until you are ready, and that is absolutely fine. Only you can decide if and when you are ready to live your Chosen Life

or you can decide to take the first step in writing your next life chapter.

I hope that reading Live Your Chosen Life has inspired you to stop and take stock of who you are and whom you need to become. I hope that by sharing my own life lessons , you can draw from them, gain confidence, and a little courage to take the steps you need to take to live a life of your own choosing.

Just remember; It's a losing game looking outside of yourself to figure out what you should be doing with your life.

No one knows but you.

Once you start to look within , the truth is that you will find the answer has been there all along. You just weren't asking the right questions to find it.

I hope we will meet one day soon when you can share all that you have achieved and more. Till then I wish you the best of success in writing your next life chapter

Blessings and much love
Saj

About The Author

Saj is the Founder and Managing Director of Institute for Change, an organisation specialising in training, coaching, and consultancy. After having defied many gender roles and stereotypes, she currently delivers her own training and coaching programs to a diverse range of organisations specialising in women empowerment, leadership, and both Personal and Professional Development.

She is the most sought-after Executive Coach for those wanting to make an empowering change in their lives. She not only works with women who are wanting to lead better lives, but also empowers them to thrive in their lives and to develop into the best version of themselves. She uses her expertise in personal development to elevate your limiting beliefs, your business, and your life to reach a greater level of success. Her USP is that she teaches "simple steps that produce dramatic and life-changing results." She seamlessly brings her integrative styled therapy techniques together, leaving her clients empowered and transformed.

Saj urges women to become champions for change. Be it their personal self and or helping other women. She has built her outstanding reputation by experiencing a lifetime of "firsts." Growing up as a Pakistani Muslim female raised by the first generation of migrants in the UK, when racism was rife and difference was abhorred, she constantly had to battle and overcome obstacles throughout her personal and professional life. She has dedicated her life to strive for equality and inclusivity to those who are disadvantaged, different, and underrepresented. She says that she is grateful for each of her "first's" because they help her understand how to help women reach their greatest potential, and live their **chosen life.**

Printed by Amazon Italia Logistica S.r.l.
Torrazza Piemonte (TO), Italy

41518760R00077